EDUCATION FOR DEMOCRACY

The Debate over the Report of the President's Commission
on Higher Education

Problems in American Civilization

READINGS SELECTED BY THE
DEPARTMENT OF AMERICAN STUDIES
AMHERST COLLEGE

Puritanism in Early America

The Causes of the American Revolution

The Declaration of Independence and the Constitution

Hamilton and the National Debt

The Turner Thesis concerning the Role of the Frontier in American History

Jackson versus Biddle — The Struggle over the Second Bank of the United States

The Transcendentalist Revolt against Materialism

Slavery as a Cause of the Civil War

Reconstruction in the South

Democracy and the Gospel of Wealth

John D. Rockefeller — Robber Baron or Industrial Statesman?

Roosevelt, Wilson, and the Trusts

Pragmatism and American Culture

The New Deal — Revolution or Evolution?

Franklin D. Roosevelt and the Supreme Court

Industry-wide Collective Bargaining — Promise or Menace?

Education for Democracy — The Debate over the Report of the President's Commission on Higher Education

Loyalty in a Democratic State

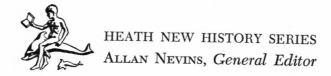

HEATH NEW HISTORY SERIES
ALLAN NEVINS, *General Editor*

EDUCATION *for* DEMOCRACY

The Debate over the Report
of the President's Commission
on Higher Education

EDITED WITH AN INTRODUCTION BY

Gail Kennedy

Problems in American Civilization

READINGS SELECTED BY THE
DEPARTMENT OF AMERICAN STUDIES
AMHERST COLLEGE

D. C. HEATH AND COMPANY: Boston

INTRODUCTION

EDUCATION is primarily concerned with the transmission and renewal of our social heritage. Its basic problem is how to bring each of the new generations to a proper maturity. But what constitutes that "maturity"? What is the *ideal* at which education should aim? In primitive societies the answer is provided by tradition. Through the example and instruction of their elders, the young receive their education in the customary way of life in that society. No alternative is or can be suggested, since, in a simple society, education is an apprenticeship to a single mode of living. It is not surprising, therefore, that the Sioux Indian boy normally turned out a good Sioux, or the Samoan Island youth a regular Samoan. In a primitive society education is omnipotent.

But our society is complex and changing. It contains every variety of social class and a multitude of different institutions. Education cannot be virtually automatic as in primitive societies. How, then, can we produce a certain sort of person, the American? That education retains, in principle, its former power is proven by the example of totalitarian countries. There is virtually no limit to what can be done to remake human nature if you have a monopoly of power over the individual's way of life. When Professor George S. Counts and Nucia P. Lodge recently published a translation of extensive excerpts from a Russian textbook on pedagogy under the title, *I Want to Be Like Stalin*, they precisely illuminated the point. To control not just the schools, of course, but all means of communication — newspapers, books, the radio — is to have the power to determine the characters of all citizens — their beliefs, their motives, and their aspirations.

What, then, is the situation with us? Have we a democratic equivalent for totalitarian education? It is clear that a democratic equivalent must be in one sense the opposite of totalitarian education. For authoritarian regimes the whole point, as in traditional societies, is to indoctrinate the individual. But in a modern democracy education has a unique function. It must not impress conformity but create attitudes that foster independence. It must rear the young to exercise freedom and accept responsibility. This is the opposite of indoctrination.

The founding fathers of our nation recognized this unique function of education in the new society they were creating. They realized that its success depended upon education in two basic ways: for the production of an enlightened public opinion and as a means of securing equality of opportunity. The first of these Washington referred to in his Farewell Address: "Promote, then, as an object of primary importance, institutions for the general diffusion of knowledge. In proportion as the structure of a government gives force to public opinion, it is essential that public opinion should be enlightened." Jefferson emphasized the other need by his proposal that free public education be provided for the ablest students from the primary school to the university. In this way he hoped to breed out of the body of the people a natural aristocracy, one elected "for genius and virtue" to serve our republic.

At the time, however, these needs were not generally recognized. Traditionally, education was a prerogative of the individual, not a duty of government. The great majority of existing schools were either philanthropic institutions, the "pauper schools," or private schools charging tuition fees. Even where schools were publicly supported, parents were usually required through "rate-bills" to pay for a part of the costs of their children's education. The struggle to overcome this traditional practice and to establish a system of universal free public education was a long and a hard one. The battle had to be fought to a finish over and over again, to break through the same barriers of apathy and prejudice, to undermine and circumvent the opposition of the same set of vested interests in every state and in every school district and municipality within that state. Indeed, one historian of education, E. P. Cubberley, says of this struggle for a public school system: "Excepting the battle for the abolition of slavery, perhaps no question has ever been before the American public for settlement which caused so much feeling or aroused such bitter antagonism."

The first campaign for free public elementary schools, waged under the generalship of leaders such as Horace Mann in Massachusetts, Henry Barnard in Connecticut, and Thaddeus Stevens in Pennsylvania, was won by the middle of the nineteenth century. But this was only the first phase of the struggle. Before it was over came the attempt to extend the system upwards by providing free secondary education through the public high school. And, finally, many states and municipalities established universities and colleges where higher education is virtually free, so far as tuition is concerned, to their citizens.

The momentum of this century-long struggle for a public school system, extending from the kindergarten to the university, has by no means been exhausted. On the contrary, with the closing of the Western frontier people came increasingly to realize that the schools are our chief remaining avenue of social mobility, that they are the foremost means of rising in the social scale. They became more and more aware also of the remaining barriers, sectional, racial, religious, and economic, to equal educational opportunity. And they have looked increasingly to the federal government to provide funds for the necessary increase of educational facilities. A recent survey conducted for *Fortune* magazine by Elmo Roper (Supplement to *Fortune*, September, 1949) showed that "eighty-three per cent of all the people would want a son of theirs (if they had one) to go to college, 69 per cent want college for their daughters." Fifty-six per cent believe that the federal government should "finance a college education for worthy students of limited means." And finally, of those who wanted their son or daughter to go to college, 66 per cent gave as their chief reason for sending a son to college, "preparation for a better job, a trade, or profession, greater earning power." (The corresponding figure for daughters was 48 per cent.)

The "G.I. Bill of Rights" under which fourteen billion dollars have been spent during the past seven years to educate eight million veterans in school or college is an outstanding confirmation of the present temper of public opinion. In his letter of appointment to the members of the President's Commission on Higher Education, President Truman explicitly referred to the strain imposed upon our colleges and universities by the immense numbers of returning veterans as one basic reason why "we should now re-examine our system of higher education in terms of its objectives, methods, and facilities; and in the light of the social role it has to play." And undoubtedly it was the response to the opportunities afforded by the "G.I. Bill" which gave the President's Commission confidence in the essential rightness of their basic proposal, the expansion upward of our system of free public education to include two more years beyond the high school.

The Commission was appointed in July, 1946. It was composed of twenty-eight distinguished American citizens under the chairmanship of George F. Zook, then President of the American Council on Education. Its report, published under the general title, *Higher Education for American Democracy*, was issued in six small volumes during the period December, 1947, to February, 1948, under the headings: Vol. I. "Establishing the Goals"; Vol. II. "Equalizing and Expanding Educational Opportunity"; Vol. III. "Organizing Higher Education"; Vol. IV. "Staffing Higher Education"; Vol. V. "Financing Higher Education"; and Vol. VI. "Resource Data" (a compilation of the statistics used in composing the Report).

One is hardly accustomed to expecting audacity from an official commission, yet the sweeping recommendations of this Report astounded conservative educationists. Clearly, the members of the Commission were impelled by the feeling that we face a crisis. They say, "In a real sense the future of our civilization depends on the direction education takes, not just in the distant future, but in the days immediately ahead" (I, 7). What they propose is the immediate abolition of all barriers to educational opportunity.

American colleges and universities must envision a much larger role for higher education in the national life. They can no longer consider themselves merely the instrument for producing an intellectual elite; they must become the means by which every citizen, youth, and adult is enabled and encouraged to carry his education, formal and informal, as far as his native capacities permit (I, 101).

To achieve this goal, they propose that we plan within the decade (by 1960) to double the enrollment in our colleges and universities. The Commission's estimate of potential enrollment by 1960 is 4,600,000 students — 2,500,000 at freshman-sophomore level, 1,-500,000 in the junior-senior years of college, and 600,000 in graduate work. This estimate is based upon the Commission's beliefs: (1) That "at least 49 per cent of our population has the mental ability to complete 14 years of schooling," while "at least 32 per cent of our population has the mental ability to complete an advanced liberal or specialized professional education" (I, 41). (2) That the great majority of those who have the ability to achieve these educational levels would wish to do so and are in fact prevented from doing so by economic handicaps, and by racial, religious, and geographical barriers.

The chief means advocated by the Commission for overcoming these handicaps are: the establishment in every state, as a part of the public school system, of "Community Colleges" which will provide easily accessible tuition-free education through the 13th and 14th grades; a federal program of scholarships "for at least 20 per cent of all undergraduate non-veteran students"; an extensive system of national fellowships for graduate study; legislation to prevent racial and religious discrimination in the selection of students; federal aid for general purposes and to enlarge the physical plant of educational institutions. On only two points were there dissents by minorities of the Commission. Four members disagreed with the Commission's forthright opposition to racial segregation in public schools (II, 29); and two Catholic members vigorously protested against the Commission's recommendation that "federal funds for current expenditures and capital outlay be appropriated for use in publicly controlled institutions of higher education only" (V, 65–68).

The controversy engendered by this Report raises many complex issues of varying degrees of importance. On a number of fundamental points the Commission has expressed opinions which represent a consensus of opinion among those who subscribe to the premises of the Report. Thus, in the readings here selected, there is a large area of agreement among proponents and critics alike. Few, if any, who believe in education *for* democracy would dispute the desirability of a generous program of federal aid to higher education, in the forms of a national system of scholarships and fellowships, an expansion of community or junior colleges, and an extensive program of adult education. And all of these liberals would favor eliminating the barriers to educational opportunity. The controversy set forth in these readings is not, therefore, over general ends but over ways and means of achieving those ends. Otherwise, there would be no common basis for an argument or any hope of eventual agreement.

Those who have commented on the Report have generally treated of several or all of the many questions involved in the order that best suited their own purposes. Hence, instead of summarizing the argument of each selection in the readings, the nature and scope of the controversy can be more clearly indicated by briefly stating the chief points at issue in their logical order. What, then, the critics (including the two dissents in the Report itself) and the Commission chiefly disagree about is:

1. *The feasibility of "higher" education for such large numbers of our youth.* Here the questions are: (a) The *political* question: Are there reactionary and antidemocratic forces which would *prevent* any such program from being put into effect? (b) What about the *financial* costs: Can we *afford* it? (c) If we can afford it, are there as many young people of college age who are really *competent* to undertake higher education: Have they the *ability?* (d) And, in any case, is the Commission right in thinking that so many of them *want* to continue their education beyond high school: Have they the *motivation?*

2. *The desirability of higher education for so great a number.* Here the chief argument is from the danger of a social and economic imbalance between *educational preparation* and *vocational opportunities.* Do we risk creating a situation where there are "millions of B.A.'s, but no jobs"?

3. *The kind, or kinds, of "higher" education which should be given.* This question brings up all the issues that have perennially

divided educators. What about the "general education" discussed and advocated by the Commission? To what *degree* should the program of higher education be *vocational* or *liberal?* Can the two be combined? If so, how? Should the program be of the *secular* kind offered in public institutions or should it have the *moral* and *religious basis* afforded by the curriculums of the church-related colleges and many other private institutions?

4. *The relation of the federal government to administration of the program.* All of the writers included in these selections agree with the Commission that the expenditure of federal grants should be made by the states. On two points, however, there is radical disagreement: Should the federal government, by using the power of withholding these funds, attempt to *compel* those states which have them to abolish their *segregation laws?* And should federal aid be restricted to *public* institutions? Do we run the risk in both cases of dangerously enhancing the *power* of the federal government? And in the second case, what will be the effects on our *private* colleges and universities? Will the *particular values* they represent be *minimized* or *destroyed?* Has the Commission devised "a procedure which will result in a totalitarianism destructive of the very democracy in which they seem to be interested"?

When the issues that confronted the Commission are analyzed in this way, it becomes obvious that a great variety of possible positions may be taken, and are taken, by the critics of the Report. But to form an opinion that is truly responsible, one should not forget the sense of crisis that animated the members of the Commission or their basic objective. In truth, three great alternatives confront the next few generations in this country: collapse, totalitarianism, or the successful maintenance of democracy. The future of democracy depends on developing individuals, in all ranks of life, who will have the ability to deal successfully with the rapid and momentous changes that are occurring in the world today. More than ever, it will be the task of the colleges to provide democratic leadership in the professions, in business, and in government. Schools, of course, cannot do everything, but they can do a great deal to mediate social change and to help us realize a full democracy.

[NOTE: The statements in "The Clash of Issues" on page x are from the following sources: Warner, Havighurst, and Loeb: *Who Shall Be Educated?* (Harper, New York, 1944); Lynd: "Who Calls the Tune?" *Journal of Higher Education,* 19 (1948), p. 166; Wickey: "The President Studies Higher Education," *Christian Education,* 31 (1948), 101–102; Gannon: *Time* magazine, Feb. 23, 1948, p. 52 (Quoted in *Time* from report of a speech); Kotschnig: *Unemployment in the Learned Professions* (Oxford University Press, London: Humphrey Milford, 1937, p. 174); The National Resources Committee, *The Problem of a Changing Population* (Government Printing Office, May, 1938, p. 221).]

CONTENTS

The Clash of Issues

A group of sociologists state the basic fact:

"Still believing that their children should rise and seeing in the secondary school and college the principal avenues of mobility, the people sent their children to secondary school and college. The American people learned what the people of older cultures have learned, that the schools are the social elevators in a hardening social structure."

— W. Lloyd Warner, Robert J. Havighurst,
and Martin B. Loeb

Others raise warning signals:

"The weakness of the 'Report of the President's Commission on Higher Education' is that it states a program for education apart from a realistic appraisal of the nature and drive of power in the contemporary United States."

— Robert S. Lynd

"It is quite evident that the basic philosophy of the Report will tend to the development of an educational program in which the state and federal control over all higher education will be so tremendous that privately-supported schools will be affected whether aided or not. In not desiring to aid through federal funds the development of any religion or denomination in its educational institutions, the Commission has gone to the other extreme of devising a procedure which will result in a totalitarianism destructive of the very democracy in which they seem to be interested."

— Gould Wickey

"By multiplying college facilities until they can care for every high school graduate who doesn't want to go to work, the commission is not doing the colleges or the country any favor. . . . How the commission hopes to multiply the sheepskins and have fewer sheep, I cannot guess. . . . This program threatens to suffocate us with tides of mediocrity."

— Very Reverend Robert I. Gannon

"In Germany the 40,000 or 50,000 workless university graduates in 1931–3 became, together with unemployed subalterns of the old imperial army, the spear-head of the national-socialist movement."

— Walter M. Kotschnig

And a government committee defines the fundamental issue:

"Education can be made a force to equalize the condition of men; it is no less true that it can be made a force to create class, race, and sectional distinctions. The evidence indicates clearly that continuance of present practices creates grave danger that our schools, which we have heretofore regarded as the bulwark of democracy, may in fact become an instrument for creating those very inequalities they were designed to prevent."

— The National Resources Committee

The President's Commission on Higher Education:
HIGHER EDUCATION FOR
AMERICAN DEMOCRACY

PRESIDENT'S COMMISSION ON HIGHER EDUCATION

GEORGE F. ZOOK, *Chairman*

SARAH G. BLANDING

O. C. CARMICHAEL

ARTHUR H. COMPTON

HENRY A. DIXON

MILTON S. EISENHOWER

JOHN R. EMENS

ALVIN C. EURICH

DOUGLAS S. FREEMAN

ALGO D. HENDERSON

Msgr. FREDERICK G. HOCHWALT

LEWIS W. JONES

HORACE M. KALLEN

FRED J. KELLY

MURRAY D. LINCOLN

T. R. MCCONNELL

EARL J. MCGRATH

MARTIN R. P. MCGUIRE

AGNES MEYER (Mrs. EUGENE)

HARRY K. NEWBURN

Bishop G. BROMLEY OXNAM

F. D. PATTERSON

MARK STARR

GEORGE D. STODDARD

HAROLD H. SWIFT

ORDWAY TEAD

GOODRICH C. WHITE

Rabbi STEPHEN S. WISE

FRANCIS J. BROWN, *Executive Secretary*

A. B. BONDS, JR., *Assistant Executive Secretary*

THE TASK OF THIS COMMISSION

THE President's Commission on Higher Education has been charged with the task of defining the responsibilities of colleges and universities in American democracy and in international affairs — and, more specifically, with reexamining the objectives, methods, and facilities of higher education in the United States in the light of the social role it has to play.

The colleges and universities themselves had begun this process of reexamination and reappraisal before the outbreak of World War II. For many years they had been healthily dissatisfied with their own accomplishments, significant though these have been. Educational leaders were troubled by an uneasy sense of shortcoming. They felt that somehow the colleges had not kept pace with changing social conditions, that the programs of higher education would have to

Reprinted from *Higher Education for Democracy: A Report of the President's Commission on Higher Education* published by Harper and Brothers.

be repatterned if they were to prepare youth to live satisfyingly and effectively in contemporary society.

One factor contributing to this sense of inadequacy has been the steadily increasing number of young people who seek a college education. As the national economy became industrialized and more complex, as production increased and national resources multiplied, the American people came in ever greater numbers to feel the need of higher education for their children. More and more American youth attended colleges and universities, but resources and equipment and curriculum did not keep pace with the growing enrollment or with the increasing diversity of needs and interests among the students.

World War II brought a temporary falling off in enrollment, but with the war's end and the enactment of Public Laws 16 and 346, the "Veterans' Rehabilitation Act," and "The G. I. Bill of Rights," the acceleration has resumed. The increase in numbers is far beyond the capacity of higher education in teachers, in buildings, and in equipment. Moreover, the number of veterans availing themselves of veterans' educational benefits falls short of the numbers that records of military personnel show could benefit from higher education. Statistics reveal that a doubling of the 1947–48 enrollment in colleges and universities will be entirely possible within 10 to 15 years, if facilities and financial means are provided.

This tendency of the American people to seek higher education in ever greater numbers has grown concurrently with an increasingly critical need for such education. To this need several developments have contributed:

(a) Science and invention have diversified natural resources, have multiplied new devices and techniques of production. These have altered in radical ways the interpersonal and intergroup relations of Americans in their work, in their play, and in their duties as citizens. As a consequence, new skills and greater maturity are required of youth as they enter upon their adult roles. And the increasing complexity that technological progress has brought to our society has made a broader understanding of social processes and problems essential for effective living.

(b) The people of America are drawn from the peoples of the entire world. They live in contrasting regions. They are of different occupations, diverse faiths, divergent cultural backgrounds, and varied interests. The American Nation is not only a union of 48 different States; it is also a union of an indefinite number of diverse groups of varying size. Of and among these diversities our free society seeks to create a dynamic unity. Where there is economic, cultural, or religious tension, we undertake to effect democratic reconciliation, so as to make of the national life one continuous process of interpersonal, intervocational, and intercultural cooperation.

(c) With World War II and its conclusion has come a fundamental shift in the orientation of American foreign policy. Owing to the inescapable pressure of events, the Nation's traditional isolationism has been displaced by a new sense of responsibility in world affairs. The need for maintaining our democracy at peace with the rest of the world has compelled our initiative in the formation of the United Nations, and America's role in this and other agencies of international cooperation requires of our citizens a knowledge of other peoples — of their political and economic systems, their social and cultural institutions —

such as has not hitherto been so urgent.

(d) The coming of the atomic age, with its ambivalent promise of tremendous good or tremendous evil for mankind, has intensified the uncertainties of the future. It has deepened and broadened the responsibilities of higher education for anticipating and preparing for the social and economic changes that will come with the application of atomic energy to industrial uses. At the same time it has underscored the need for education and research for the self-protection of our democracy, for demonstrating the merits of our way of life to other peoples.

Thus American colleges and universities face the need both for improving the performance of their traditional tasks and for assuming the new tasks created for them by the new internal conditions and external relations under which the American people are striving to live and to grow as a free people.

It is against the background of these conditions that the President's Commission has been called upon to reexamine higher education in the United States. In doing this, the Commission has undertaken to appraise our most urgent national needs, to define in terms of those needs the major goals toward which higher education should move, and to indicate certain changes in educational policy and program which it considers necessary for the attainment of these goals. . . .

EDUCATION FOR A BETTER NATION AND A BETTER WORLD

Education is an institution of every civilized society, but the purposes of education are not the same in all societies. An educational system finds its guiding principles and ultimate goals in the aims

and philosophy of the social order in which it functions. The two predominant types of society in the world today are the democratic and the authoritarian, and the social role of education is very different in the two systems.

American society is a democracy: that is, its folkways and institutions, its arts and sciences and religions are based on the principle of equal freedom and equal rights for all its members, regardless of race, faith, sex, occupation, or economic status. The law of the land, providing equal justice for the poor as well as the rich, for the weak as well as the strong, is one instrument by which a democratic society establishes, maintains, and protects this equality among different persons and groups. The other instrument is education, which, as all the leaders in the making of democracy have pointed out again and again, is necessary to give effect to the equality prescribed by law.

THE ROLE OF EDUCATION

It is a commonplace of the democratic faith that education is indispensable to the maintenance and growth of freedom of thought, faith, enterprise, and association. Thus the social role of education in a democratic society is at once to insure equal liberty and equal opportunity to differing individuals and groups, and to enable the citizens to understand, appraise, and redirect forces, men, and events as these tend to strengthen or to weaken their liberties.

In performing this role, education will necessarily vary its means and methods to fit the diversity of its constituency, but it will achieve its ends more successfully if its programs and policies grow out of and are relevant to the characteristics and needs of contemporary society. Effective democratic education will deal directly with current problems.

This is not to say that education should neglect the past — only that it should not get lost in the past. No one would deny that a study of man's history can contribute immeasurably to understanding and managing the present. But to assume that all we need do is apply to present and future problems "eternal" truths revealed in earlier ages is likely to stifle creative imagination and intellectual daring. Such an assumption may blind us to new problems and the possible need for new solutions. It is wisdom in education to use the past selectively and critically, in order to illumine the pressing problems of the present.

At the same time education is the making of the future. Its role in a democratic society is that of critic and leader as well as servant; its task is not merely to meet the demands of the present but to alter those demands if necessary, so as to keep them always suited to democratic ideals. Perhaps its most important role is to serve as an instrument of social transition, and its responsibilities are defined in terms of the kind of civilization society hopes to build. If its adjustments to present needs are not to be mere fortuitous improvisations, those who formulate its policies and programs must have a vision of the Nation and the world we want — to give a sense of direction to their choices among alternatives.

What America needs today, then, is "a schooling better aware of its aims." Our colleges need to see clearly what it is they are trying to accomplish. The efforts of individual institutions, local communities, the several States, the educational foundations and associations, and the Federal Government will all be more effective if they are directed toward the same general ends.

In the future as in the past, American higher education will embody the prin- *ciple of diversity in unity: each institution, State, or other agency will continue to make its own contribution in its own way. But educational leaders should try to agree on certain common objectives that can serve as a stimulus and guide to individual decision and action.*

A TIME OF CRISIS

It is essential today that education come decisively to grips with the world-wide crisis of mankind. This is no careless or uncritical use of words. No thinking person doubts that we are living in a decisive moment of human history.

Atomic scientists are doing their utmost to make us realize how easily and quickly a world catastrophe may come. They know the fearful power for destruction possessed by the weapons their knowledge and skill have fashioned. They know that the scientific principles on which these weapons are based are no secret to the scientists of other nations, and that America's monopoly of the engineering processes involved in the manufacture of atom bombs is not likely to last many years. And to the horror of atomic weapons, biological and chemical instruments of destruction are now being added.

But disaster is not inevitable. The release of atomic energy that has brought man within sight of world devastation has just as truly brought him the promise of a brighter future. The potentialities of atomic power are as great for human betterment as for human annihilation. Man can choose which he will have.

The possibility of this choice is the supreme fact of our day, and it will necessarily influence the ordering of educational priorities. We have a big job of re-education to do. Nothing less than a complete reorientation of our thinking will suffice if mankind is to survive and move on to higher levels.

In a real sense the future of our civilization depends on the direction education takes, not just in the distant future, but in the days immediately ahead.

This crisis is admittedly world-wide. All nations need reeducation to meet it. But this fact does not lessen the obligation of colleges and universities to undertake the task in the United States. On the contrary, our new position in international affairs increases the obligation. We can do something about the problem in our own country and in occupied areas, and hope that by so doing we will win the friendly cooperation of other nations.

The fundamental goal of the United States in its administration of occupied areas must be the reeducation of the populations to the individual responsibilities of democracy. Such reeducation calls for the immediate removal of authoritarian barriers to democratic education, and inculcation of democratic ideals and principles through the guidance, example, and wisdom of United States occupation forces. The primacy of the objective of reeducation, however, appears too often to have been lost sight of in the press of day-to-day administrative problems. Yet every contact by Americans with Germans or Japanese either strengthens or retards the achievement of the goal. Evidence reaching this Commission indicates that while many specific existing barriers to democratic reform have been removed, new obstacles are being created daily by inadequacies of educational personnel and policy. Cognizant of the great responsibility of American education to promote democratic ideals in occupied areas, this Commission recommends the formation of a special committee to appraise progress and offer advice to the Departments of State and National Defense on educational policy and administration in occupied areas.

The schools and colleges are not solely or even mainly to blame for the situation in which we find ourselves, or that the responsibility for resolving the crisis is not or can not be entirely theirs. But the scientific knowledge and technical skills that have made atomic and bacteriological warfare possible are the products of education and research, and higher education must share proportionately in the task of forging social and political defenses against obliteration. The indirect way toward some longer view and superficial curricular tinkering can no longer serve. The measures higher education takes will have to match in boldness and vision the magnitude of the problem.

In the light of this situation, the President's Commission on Higher Education has attempted to select, from among the principal goals for higher education, those which should come first in our time. They are to bring to all the people of the Nation:

Education for a fuller realization of democracy in every phase of living.

Education directly and explicitly for international understanding and cooperation.

Education for the application of creative imagination and trained intelligence to the solution of social problems and to the administration of public affairs.

TOWARD A FULLER REALIZATION OF DEMOCRACY

The dramatic events of the last few years have tended to focus our attention on the need for a world view, for global vision, for international-mindedness. This is an urgent necessity, but it would be unwise to let this necessity blind us to the fact that America's leadership in world affairs can be effective only as it rests upon increasing strength and unity at home.

Understanding Among Men

Harmony and cooperation among peoples of differing races, customs, and opinions is not one thing on the regional or national level and another on the international. The problem of understanding among men is indivisible, and the mutual acceptance and respect upon which any reliable international cooperation must depend, begin at home.

If we cannot reconcile conflicts of opinion and interest among the diverse groups that make up our own Nation, we are not likely to succeed in compromising the differences that divide nations. If we cannot make scientific and technological progress contribute to the greater well-being of all our own citizens, we shall scarcely be able to exercise leadership in reducing inequality and injustice among the other peoples of the world. If we cannot achieve a fuller realization of democracy in the United States, we are not likely to secure its adoption willingly outside the United States.

A century ago even political thinkers who did not approve the trend toward democracy accepted its eventual triumph as inevitable. Today we cannot be so sure that the future of the democratic way of life is secure. Within recent decades democratic principles have been dangerously challenged by authoritarianism, and World War II did not by any means resolve the conflict. The issue of a free society versus totalitarianism is still very much with us. It has been called "the critical and supreme political issue of today."

It is the American faith that the ultimate verdict in this conflict will go to that form of human association and government which best serves the needs and promotes the welfare of the people. We firmly believe that democracy is this form, but we shall convince others only by demonstration, not by words.

It is certainly to be hoped that we of America will continue to give democracy, and not its opponents, our full moral and economic support wherever efforts toward freedom appear, but we can do most to strengthen and extend the democratic ideal in the world by increasing the vigor and effectiveness of our achievement at home. Only to the extent that we make our own democracy function to improve the physical and mental well-being of our citizens can we hope to see freedom grow, not vanish, from the earth.

"To preserve our democracy we must improve it." Surely this fact determines one of today's urgent objectives for higher education. In the past our colleges have perhaps taken it for granted that education for democratic living could be left to courses in history and political science. It should become instead a primary aim of all classroom teaching and, more important still, of every phase of campus life.

Development of the Individual

The first goal in education for democracy is the full, rounded, and continuing development of the person. The discovery, training, and utilization of individual talents is of fundamental importance in a free society. To liberate and perfect the intrinsic powers of every citizen is the central purpose of democracy, and its furtherance of individual self-realization is its greatest glory.

A free society is necessarily composed of free citizens, and men are not made free solely by the absence of external restraints. Freedom is a function of the mind and the spirit. It flows from strength of character, firmness of conviction, integrity of purpose. It is channeled by knowledge, understanding, and the exercise of discriminating judgment. It consists of freedom of thought and conscience in action. Free men are men who not only insist on rights and liberties but who of their own free will assume the corresponding responsibilities and obligations.

If our colleges and universities are to graduate individuals who have learned how to be free, they will have to concern themselves with the development of self-discipline and self-reliance, of ethical principles as a guide for conduct, of sensitivity to injustice and inequality, of insight into human motives and aspirations, of discriminating appreciation of a wide range of human values, of the spirit of democratic compromise and cooperation.

Responsibility for the development of these personal qualities cannot be left as heretofore to some courses or a few departments or scattered extracurricular organizations; it must become a part of every phase of college life.

Social Responsibility

Higher education has always attempted to teach young people both spiritual and material values. The classroom has imparted the principle of collective responsibility for liberty — the rule that no one person's right to freedom can be maintained unless all men work together to make secure the freedom of all.

But these efforts have not always been effective. All too often the benefits of education have been sought and used for personal and private profit, to the neglect of public and social service. Yet individual freedom entails communal responsibility. The democratic way of life can endure only as private careers and social obligations are made to mesh, as personal ambition is reconciled with public responsibility.

Today, all are agreed, we need as never before to enlist all the abilities and energies we can command in the conduct of our common affairs. Today less than ever can we afford the social loss that occurs when educated men and women neglect their obligations as citizens and deliberately refrain from taking part in public affairs.

To preserve everybody's right to life, liberty, and the pursuit of happiness, then, we need first to become aware of the fact that there is no longer room for isolationism in any successful life, personal or national. No man can live to himself alone, expecting to benefit from social progress without contributing to it.

Nor can any *group* in our society, organized or unorganized, pursue purely private ends and seek to promote its own welfare without regard to the social consequences of its activities. Business, industry, labor, agriculture, medicine, law, engineering, education . . . all these modes of association call for the voluntary development of codes of conduct, or the revision of such codes as already exist, to harmonize the special interests of the group with the general welfare.

Toward these ends, higher education must inspire its graduates with high social aims as well as endow them with specialized information and technical skill. Teaching and learning must be invested with public purpose. . . .

IT CAN BE DONE

In emphasizing education for democracy, for international understanding, and for more effective social science as objectives for higher education in America today, the President's Commission has no desire to suggest limitations on progress and experimentation in other directions. Diversity in purpose is a potential source of strength in democratic institutions. From the innovation and experimental approach of today may well come the general objective of tomorrow.

These three goals are stated as the minimum essentials of the program to be developed in all institutions of higher education. And they pose a truly staggering job for the colleges and universities. But it can be done. The necessary intelligence and ability exist. What we need is awareness of the urgency of the task, the will and the courage to tackle it, and wholehearted commitment to its successful performance.

But to delay is to fail. Colleges must accelerate the normally slow rate of social change which the educational system reflects; we need to find ways quickly of making the understanding and vision of our most farsighted and sensitive citizens the common possession of all our people.

To this end the educational task is partly a matter of the numbers to be educated and partly one of the kind of education to be provided. We shall have to educate more of our people at each level of the educational program, and we shall have to devise patterns of education that will prepare them more effectively than in the past for responsible roles in modern society. . . .

EDUCATION FOR ALL

Education is by far the biggest and the most hopeful of the Nation's enterprises. Long ago our people recognized that education for all is not only democracy's obligation but its necessity. Education is the foundation of democratic liberties. Without an educated citizenry alert to preserve and extend freedom, it would not long endure.

Accepting this truth, the United States has devoted many of its best minds and billions of its wealth to the development and maintenance of an extensive system of free public schools, and through the years the level of schooling attained by more and more of our people has steadily risen.

RECORD OF GROWTH

The expansion of the American educational enterprise since the turn of the century has been phenomenal. The 700,000 enrollment in high schools in the school year 1900 was equal to only 11 percent of the youth of usual high-school age, 14 through 17 years old. This increased in 1940 to over 7,000,000 students representing 73 per cent of the youth.

Almost as spectacular has been the increase in college attendance. In 1900 fewer than 250,000 students, only 4 percent of the population 18 through 21 years of age, were enrolled in institutions of higher education. By 1940 the enrollment had risen to 1,500,000 students, equal to a little less than 16 percent of the 18–21 year olds. In 1947, enrollments jumped to the theretofore unprecedented peak of 2,354,000 although approximately 1,000,000 of the students were veterans, older than the usual college age because World War II had deferred their education. The situation in the fall of 1947 gives every indication that the school year 1948 will witness even larger enrollments.

This record of growth is encouraging, but we are forced to admit nonetheless that the educational attainments of the American people are still substantially below what is necessary either for effective individual living or for the welfare of our society.

According to the U. S. Bureau of the Census, almost 17,000,000 men and women over 19 years of age in 1947 had stopped their schooling at the sixth grade or less. Of these, 9,000,000 had never attended school or had stopped their schooling before completing the fifth grade. In 1947, about 1,600,000 or 19 percent of our high-school-age boys and girls were not attending any kind of school, and over two-thirds of the 18- and 19-year-old youths were not in school.

These are disturbing facts. They represent a sobering failure to reach the educational goals implicit in the democratic creed, and they are indefensible in a society so richly endowed with material resources as our own. We cannot allow so many of our people to remain so ill equipped either as human beings or as citizens of a democracy.

Great as the total American expenditure for education may seem, we have not been devoting any really appreciable part of our vast wealth to higher education. As table 1 shows, even though in the last 15 years our annual budget for education has risen in number of dollars, it has actually declined in relation to our increasing economic productivity.

The $1,000,000,000 we have put into our colleges and universities in 1947 was less than one-half of 1 percent of the gross national product, which is the market value of all the goods and services produced in the country in that year.

TABLE 1 — *Direct Cost of Higher Education and Its Relation to the Gross National Product*

Fiscal year	Amount (in millions)*	Proportion of gross national product (percent)†
1932	$ 421	0.63
1940	522	.55
1947	1,005	.46

* Source: General and educational expenditures, not including capital expansion, as reported by U. S. Office of Education.

† Source of gross national product: U. S. Bureau of Foreign and Domestic Commerce.

BARRIERS TO EQUAL OPPORTUNITY

One of the gravest charges to which American society is subject is that of failing to provide a reasonable equality of educational opportunity for its youth. For the great majority of our boys and girls, the kind and amount of education they may hope to attain depends, not on their own abilities, but on the family or community into which they happened to be born or, worse still, on the color of their skin or the religion of their parents.

Economic Barriers

The old, comfortable idea that "any boy can get a college education who has it in him" simply is not true. Low family income, together with the rising costs of education, constitutes an almost impassable barrier to college education for many young people. For some, in fact, the barrier is raised so early in life that it prevents them from attending high school even when free public high schools exist near their homes.

Despite the upward trend in average per capita income for the past century and more, the earnings of a large part of our population are still too low to provide anything but the barest necessities of physical life. It is a distressing fact that in 1945, when the total national income was far greater than in any previous period in our history, half of the children under 18 were growing up in families which had a cash income of $2,530 or less. The educational significance of these facts is heightened by the relationship that exists between income and birth rate. Fertility is highest in the families with lowest incomes.

In the elementary and secondary schools the effects of these economic conditions are overcome to a considerable extent, though not entirely, by the fact that education is free and at certain ages is compulsory. But this does not hold true at the college level. For a number of years the tendency has been for the college student to bear an increasing share of the cost of his own education. Even in State-supported institutions we have been moving away from the principle of free education to a much greater degree than is commonly supposed.

Under the pressure of rising costs and of a relative lessening of public support, the colleges and universities are having to depend more and more on tuition fees to meet their budgets. As a result, on the average, tuition rates rose about 30 percent from 1939 to 1947.

Nor are tuition costs the whole of it. There are not enough colleges and universities in the country, and they are not distributed evenly enough to bring them within reach of all young people. Relatively few students can attend college in their home communities. So to the expense of a college education for most youth must be added transportation and living costs — by no means a small item.

This economic factor explains in large part why the father's occupation has been found in many studies to rank so high as a determining factor in a young person's college expectancy. A farm laborer earns less than a banker or a doctor, for instance, and so is less able to afford the costs of higher education for his children. The children, moreover, have less inducement to seek a college education because of their family background. In some social circles a college education is often considered a luxury which can be done without, something desirable perhaps, "but not for the likes of us."

The importance of economic barriers to post-high school education lies in the fact that there is little if any relationship between the ability to benefit from a college education and the ability to pay for it. Studies discussed in the volume of this Commission's report, "Equalizing and Ex-

panding Individual Opportunity," show that among children of equally high ability those with fathers in higher-income occupations had greater probability of attending college.

By allowing the opportunity for higher education to depend so largely on the individual's economic status, we are not only denying to millions of young people the chance in life to which they are entitled; we are also depriving the Nation of a vast amount of potential leadership and potential social competence which it sorely needs.

Regional Variations

An individual's birthplace may also determine how much and what kind of an education he is likely to get. Regional differences are largely caused by differentials in wealth and human fertility. There is a tremendous variation in per capita wealth from State to State and even among counties within a State. And the poorer areas tend to have a larger proportion of young people to adults. Consequently the unequal distribution of children in relation to income represents an unequal distribution of the Nation's bill for education.

Where a community or State with a low income has an extremely high birth rate, it becomes next to impossible for it to provide the funds for an adequate educational program. In contrast, communities with a relatively small youth population are in a far better position to meet their obligation. In 1945, for example, only 18 percent of the population of California was between 5–17 years of age. In the same year, the 5–17 year age group amounted to 31 percent of the population of South Carolina. As a measure of potential support for the schools, the total income payments in each State was divided by the number of children in that State. The results of this appraisal are shown in table 2. If California's percentage of children had been as high as South Carolina's, the State income per child of school age would have been cut from $9,029 to $5,243. If South Carolina's percentage of youth had been as low as California's, her State income per child would have been raised from $2,363 to $4,070.

By devoting 1.5 percent of the 1945 income in the State to public elementary and secondary education, California managed an average expenditure per child of $131, whereas 1.8 percent of the total income in Mississippi averaged $36 per child. If Mississippi had equaled California's educational expenditures per child, it would have consumed 6.5 cents out of every dollar of income received by every person in Mississippi. The resulting inequality of educational opportunity for the children of the two States is glaringly obvious.

TABLE 2 — *Income Per Child of School Age by States: 1945°*

State	Income payments to individual per child 5–17 in 1945
California	$9,029
New York	8,674
Washington	8,202
Connecticut	7,819
Montana	7,545
Nevada	7,466
New Jersey	7,323
Illinois	7,142
Oregon	7,109
Massachusetts	6,915
Delaware	6,854
Rhode Island	6,770
Ohio	6,432
Maryland	5,784
Indiana	5,640
Michigan	5,638
Pennsylvania	5,582
Florida	5,320
Kansas	5,227
Wisconsin	5,200
Colorado	5,109
Missouri	5,082

State	Income payments to individual per child 5–17 in 1945
Nebraska	5,066
Wyoming	5,006
District of Columbia	4,939
Iowa	4,826
New Hampshire	4,806
Minnesota	4,779
Maine	4,538
Vermont	4,503
South Dakota	4,500
Idaho	4,362
Texas	4,119
Utah	4,058
Arizona	3,864
North Dakota	3,855
Virginia	3,693
Oklahoma	3,429
Tennessee	3,282
Louisiana	3,238
West Virginia	2,906
Georgia	2,903
New Mexico	2,838
Kentucky	2,780
North Carolina	2,671
Alabama	2,534
Arkansas	2,498
South Carolina	2,363
Mississippi	2,018

° Source of income data is income payments to individuals as reported by the U. S. Bureau of Foreign and Domestic Commerce; data on children 5–17 years of age from the U. S. Bureau of the Census.

For a long period, the South has had a higher proportion of its population in the younger ages.

TABLE 3 — *Distribution of Civilian Population, Births, and School Age Children by Geographic Regions: 1945*

Region	Civilian population° Percent	Births† Percent	Children aged 5 through 17° Percent
United States	100.0	100.0	100.0
Northeast	26.5	23.5	23.7
Northcentral	30.2	27.9	28.3
South	31.1	35.8	37.1
West	12.2	12.8	10.9

° Source: U. S. Bureau of the Census.
† Source: National Office of Vital Statistics.

In 1945, the South had 27.0 percent of its population in the ages 5 through 17, as contrasted with a national average of 22.7 percent and with 20.2 percent in the Northeast. In that year, the South had a birth rate of 24.7 per 1,000 civilians while the Nation averaged 21.5 and the Northeast had only 19.0 births per thousand civilians. Clearly the South is supplying new population to the Nation out of all proportion to its numbers.

Sharp and significant differences exist between the educational situations in urban and rural areas. For example, with respect to the educational attainment of youths aged 20 to 24, the median of school years completed in 1940 was 12.0 in urban areas, 10.7 in rural nonfarm areas and 8.8 in rural farm areas. The same disparity is revealed in the analysis of schooling completed by the adult population, shown in table 4.

TABLE 4 — *Proportion of Population 25 Years Old and Older Completing Selected Levels of Schooling: 1940°*

Schooling completed	Urban areas	Rural nonfarm areas	Rural farm areas
	Percent	Percent	Percent
4 years or more of college	5.7	4.2	1.3
Less than 5 years of grade school	11.2	13.6	20.4

° Source: U. S. Bureau of the Census.

Thus, it is apparent that, just before World War II, a man or woman living on a farm had only about one-fourth the chance of having completed college as someone in the city, and almost twice as much chance of not having completed more than 4 years of grade school. In 1947, of the urban youth 20 to 24 years of age, 12.5 percent were attending school, whereas of the rural nonfarm youth 8.8 percent were in school, and of the farm youth only 6.5 percent were in

school. Thus, it appears as though much of this differential is persisting.

It is all too clear that whether one considers regional variations or urban-rural differentials, the fact is that the future citizens of the Nation are being born in disproportionately large numbers in communities in which economic resources are the weakest, the plane of living the lowest, cultural conditions the poorest, and the home the least well equipped to contribute either to the physical well-being of youth or to their intellectual development.

These conditions mean that millions of youth are being denied their just right to an adequate education. The accident of being born in one place rather than another ought not to affect so profoundly a young person's chance of getting an education commensurate with his native capacities.

But the situation has even deeper meaning in its implications for society. Educational leaders must squarely face the fact that the unequal distribution of children in relation to regional and urban-rural differences in wealth is tending to cancel out the potential benefits of our educational enterprise. The greater number of children being born in the families and the regions of the country that are least able to provide them with a good education at home or in school is contributing to the spread of a meager cultural heritage, and this may one day tip the balance in our struggle for a better civilization.

No one would suggest that the proper remedy for this situation is a lower birth rate in any part of the country. America's children are America's most vital resource.

The only possible solution of the problem is, as rapidly as possible, to raise economic and cultural levels in our less advanced areas, and in the

meantime to provide outside assistance that will enable these areas to give their children equal educational opportunities with all others in the Nation.

Barrier of a Restricted Curriculum

We shall be denying educational opportunity to many young people as long as we maintain the present orientation of higher education toward verbal skills and intellectual interests. Many young people have abilities of a different kind, and they cannot receive "education commensurate with their native capacities" in colleges and universities that recognize only one kind of educable intelligence.

Traditionally the colleges have sifted out as their special clientele persons possessing verbal aptitudes and a capacity for grasping abstractions. But many other aptitudes — such as social sensitivity and versatility, artistic ability, motor skill and dexterity, and mechanical aptitude and ingenuity — also should be cultivated in a society depending, as ours does, on the minute division of labor and at the same time upon the orchestration of an enormous variety of talents.

If the colleges are to educate the great body of American youth, they must provide programs for the development of other abilities than those involved in academic aptitude, and they cannot continue to concentrate on students with one type of intelligence to the neglect of youth with other talents.

Racial and Religious Barriers

The outstanding example of these barriers to equal opportunity, of course, is the disadvantages suffered by our Negro citizens. The low educational attainments of Negro adults reflect the cumulative effects of a long period of unequal opportunity. In 1940 the schooling of the Negro was significantly below that of whites at every level from the first grade through college. At the college level, the difference is marked; 11 percent of the white population 20 years of age and over had completed at least 1 year of college and almost 5 percent had finished 4 years; whereas for the nonwhites (over 95 percent of whom are Negroes) only a little more than 3 percent had completed at least 1 year of college and less than 1½ percent had completed a full course.

Gains Have Been Made. Noteworthy advances have been made toward eliminating the racial inequalities which in large measure are responsible for this low level of educational achievement by the Negroes. Between 1900 and 1940 the percentage of Negroes 5 to 20 years of age attending school rose from 31.0 percent to 64.4 percent. And the percentage of Negro youth 15 to 20 years old attending school increased from 17.5 in 1900 to 33.8 in 1940. That differentials still persist, however, is shown in table 5.

TABLE 5 — *Proportion of Young Persons Attending School, by Age and Color: April 1947* *

| | Attending school | |
| | White | Nonwhites (about 95 percent Negro) |
Age		
	Percent	*Percent*
6 years of age...........	67.8	63.4
7 to 9 years of age.......	97.1	89.2
10 to 13 years of age.....	98.2	93.7
14 to 17 years of age.....	82.5	71.9
18 to 19 years of age.....	28.2	24.2
20 to 24 years of age.....	11.3	6.7

* Source: U. S. Bureau of the Census.

Institutions which accept both Negro and non-Negro students do not maintain separate record systems for Negroes, and so data on enrollment of Negroes are restricted to those institutions — usually located in the South — which accept only

Negro students. In recent years, since 1932, these institutions have almost tripled their enrollments whereas the institutions for whites or which are unsegregated only about doubled theirs:

TABLE 6 — *Enrollment of Institutions of Higher Education and Index of Change**

	Enrollments in institutions accepting			
	Negroes only		All others	
		Index of		Index of
Year	Number	change	Number	change
		(1932=100)		(1932=100)
1932	21,880	100	1,132,237	100
1936	32,628	149	1,175,599	104
1940	41,839	191	1,452,364	128
1947†	63,500	290	2,290,500	202

* Source is resident enrollment as reported by U. S. Office of Education.
† Estimated.

Inequalities Remain. But the numbers enrolled in school do not tell the whole story. Marked as has been the progress in Negro education in recent years, it cannot obscure the very great differences which still persist in educational opportunities afforded the Negro and the non-Negro.

In 17 States and the District of Columbia, segregation of the Negroes in education is established by law.[1] In the *Gaines* decision, the U. S. Supreme Court ruled that "if a State furnishes higher education to white residents, it is bound to furnish [within the State] substantially equal advantages to Negro students." Although segregation may not legally mean discrimination as to the quality of the facilities it usually does so in fact.

[1] In the case of *Mendez* v. *Westminster School District,* the segregation of students of Mexican ancestry in the Westminster, Calif., school district, on the alleged grounds that because of their ancestry such students have language difficulties, was held illegal. The U. S. district court which heard the case held that segregation is unconstitutional under the Federal Constitution. On appeal by the Westminster school district, the U. S. circuit court of appeals limited its affirmance of the district court's decision by holding that the specific statutes involved were illegal under California law.

The schools maintained for the Negroes are commonly much inferior to those for the whites. The Negro schools are financed at a pitifully low level, they are often housed in buildings wholly inadequate for the purpose, and many of the teachers are sorely in need of more education themselves. Library facilities are generally poor or lacking altogether, and professional supervision is more a name than a reality.

These facts are supported strongly by a recent study in the District of Columbia. The District's Superintendent of Schools in his 1946–47 report to the Board of Education states that the student-teacher ratios in the schools for Negroes were significantly and consistently higher than those for non-Negroes — from the kindergartens through the teachers' colleges.

Segregation lessens the quality of education for the whites as well. To maintain two school systems side by side — duplicating even inadequately the buildings, equipment, and teaching personnel — means that neither can be of the quality that would be possible if all the available resources were devoted to one system, especially not when the States least able financially to support an adequate educational program for their youth are the very ones that are trying to carry a double load.

It must not be supposed that Negro youth living in States in which segregation is not legalized are given the same opportunites as white youth. In these areas economic and social discrimination of various sorts often operates to produce segregation in certain neighborhoods, which are frequently characterized by poorer school buildings, less equipment and less able teachers.

Equality of educational opportunity is not achieved by the mere physical

existence of schools; it involves also the quality of teaching and learning that takes place in them.

The Quota System. At the college level a different form of discrimination is commonly practiced. *Many colleges and universities, especially in their professional schools, maintain a selective quota system for admission, under which the chance to learn, and thereby to become more useful citizens, is denied to certain minorities, particularly to Negroes and Jews.*

This practice is a violation of a major American principle and is contributing to the growing tension in one of the crucial areas of our democracy.

The quota, or *numerous clausus,* is certainly un-American. It is European in origin and application, and we have lately witnessed on that continent the horrors to which, in its logical extension, it can lead. To insist that specialists in any field shall be limited by ethnic quotas is to assume that the Nation is composed of separate and self-sufficient ethnic groups and this assumption America has never made except in the case of its Negro population, where the result is one of the plainest inconsistencies with our national ideal.

The quota system denies the basic American belief that intelligence and ability are present in all ethnic groups, that men of all religious and racial origins should have equal opportunity to fit themselves for contributing to the common life.

Moreover, since the quota system is never applied to all groups in the Nation's population, but only to certain ones, we are forced to conclude that the arguments advanced to justify it are nothing more than rationalizations to cover either convenience or the disposi-

tion to discriminate. The quota system cannot be justified on any grounds compatible with democratic principles.

Consequences of Inequalities of Opportunity

These various barriers to educational opportunity involve grave consequences both for the individual and for society.

From the viewpoint of the individual they are denying to millions of young people what the democratic creed assumes to be their birthright: an equal chance with all others to make the most of their native abilities. From the viewpoint of society the barriers mean that far too few of our young people are getting enough preparation for assuming the personal, social, and civic responsibilities of adults living in a democratic society.

It is especially serious that not more of our most talented young people continue their schooling beyond high school in this day when the complexity of life and of our social problems means that we need desperately every bit of trained intelligence we can assemble. The present state of affairs is resulting in far too great a loss of talent — our most precious natural resource in a democracy.

In a country as vast as the United States, with all its regional differences in cultural patterns and economic resources, absolute equality of educational opportunity perhaps may not be reasonably expected. But today the differences that do exist are so great as to compel immediate action.

In communities where the birth rate is low, where the burden of caring for the nurture and education of the oncoming generation is relatively light, where the level of living is high, the advantages of education are extended to youth on more nearly equal terms. But in communities where the birth rate is high, where the economic structure is weak, where the level of living is low, where community and family resources contribute least to intellectual growth, there we support education in niggardly fashion, though at great effort.

If over the years we continue to draw the population reserves of the Nation from the most underprivileged areas and families and fail to make good the deficit by adequate educational opportunities, we shall be following a course that is sure to prove disastrous to the level of our culture and to the whole fabric of our democratic institutions.

We have proclaimed our faith in education as a means of equalizing the conditions of men. But there is grave danger that our present policy will make it an instrument for creating the very inequalities it was designed to prevent. If the ladder of educational opportunity rises high at the doors of some youth and scarcely rises at all at the doors of others, while at the same time formal education is made a prerequisite to occupational and social advance, then education may become the means, not of eliminating race and class distinctions, but of deepening and solidifying them.

It is obvious, then, that free and universal access to education, in terms of the interest, ability, and need of the student, must be a major goal in American education.

TOWARD EQUALIZING OPPORTUNITY

The American people should set as their ultimate goal an educational system in which at no level — high school, college, graduate school, or professional school — will a qualified individual in any part of the country encounter an insuperable economic barrier to the attainment of the kind of education suited to his aptitudes and interests.

This means that we shall aim at making higher education equally available to all young people, as we now do education in the elementary and high schools, to the extent that their capacity warrants a further social investment in their training.

Obviously this desirable realization of our ideal of equal educational opportunity cannot be attained immediately. But if we move toward it as fast as our economic resources permit, it should not lie too far in the future. Technological advances, that are already resulting in phenomenal increases in productivity per worker, promise us a degree of economic well-being that would have seemed wholly Utopian to our fathers. With wise management of our economy, we shall almost certainly be able to support education at all levels far more adequately in the future than we could in the past.

The Commission recommends that steps be taken to reach the following objectives without delay:

1. High school education must be improved and should be provided for all normal youth.

This is a minimum essential. We cannot safely permit any of our citizens for any reason other than incapacity, to stop short of a high school education or its equivalent. To achieve the purpose of such education, however, it must be improved in facilities and in the diversity of its curriculum. Better high school education is essential, both to raise the caliber of students entering college and to provide the best training possible for those who end their formal education with the twelfth grade.

2. The time has come to make education through the fourteenth grade available in the same way that high school education is now available.

This means that tuition-free education

should be available in public institutions to all youth for the traditional freshman and sophomore years or for the traditional 2-year junior college course.

To achieve this, it will be necessary to develop much more extensively than at present such opportunities as are now provided in local communities by the 2-year junior college, community institute, community college, or institute of arts and sciences. The name used does not matter, though community college seems to describe these schools best; the important thing is that the services they perform be recognized and vastly extended.

Such institutions make post–high school education available to a much larger percentage of young people than otherwise could afford it. Indeed, as discussed in the volume of this Commission's report, "Organizing Higher Education," such community colleges probably will have to carry a large part of the responsibility for expanding opportunities in higher education.

3. The time has come to provide financial assistance to competent students in the tenth through fourteenth grades who would not be able to continue their education without such assistance.

Tuition costs are not the major economic barrier to education, especially in college. Costs of supplies, board, and room, and other living needs are great. Even many high-school students are unable to continue in school because of these costs.

Arrangements must be made, therefore, to provide additional financial assistance for worthy students who need it if they are to remain in school. Only in this way can we counteract the effect of family incomes so low that even tuition-free schooling is a financial impossibility for their children. Only in this way

can we make sure that all who are to participate in democracy are adequately prepared to do so.

4. The time has come to reverse the present tendency of increasing tuition and other student fees in the senior college beyond the fourteenth year, and in both graduate and professional schools, by lowering tuition costs in publicly controlled colleges and by aiding deserving students through inaugurating a program of scholarships and fellowships.

Only in this way can we be sure that economic and social barriers will not prevent the realization of the promise that lies in our most gifted youth. Only in this way can we be certain of developing for the common good all the potential leadership our society produces, no matter in what social or economic stratum it appears.

5. The time has come to expand considerably our program of adult education, and to make more of it the responsibility of our colleges and universities.

The crisis of the time and the rapidly changing conditions under which we live make it especially necessary that we provide a continuing and effective educational program for adults as well as youth. We can in this way, perhaps, make up some of the educational deficiencies of the past, and also in a measure counteract the pressures and distractions of adult life that all too often make the end of formal schooling the end of education too.

6. The time has come to make public education at all levels equally accessible to all, without regard to race, creed, sex or national origin.

If education is to make the attainment of a more perfect democracy one of its major goals, it is imperative that it extend its benefits to all on equal terms.

It must renounce the practices of discrimination and segregation in educational institutions as contrary to the spirit of democracy. Educational leaders and institutions should take positive steps to overcome the conditions which at present obstruct free and equal access to educational opportunities. Educational programs everywhere should be aimed at undermining and eventually eliminating the attitudes that are responsible for discrimination and segregation — at creating instead attitudes that will make education freely available to all.[2]

NUMBER WHO SHOULD RECEIVE HIGHER EDUCATION

Achieving these immediate objectives necessarily will require a tremendous expansion of our educational enterprise at the college level.

It will be noted that many of the Commission's projects focus upon the year 1960. There are several important reasons why the Commission has chosen to look this far ahead. First of all, in the President's letter of appointment, the Commission was asked to direct its energies toward the investigation of long-term policy issues in American higher education. The Commission itself selected the terminal date of 1960 since it was felt that manageable data could be procured for studies up to this point. The basic consideration of population data weighed heavily in the selection. Individuals who will be enrolled in colleges in 1960 through 1964 have already been born,

[2] The following Commission members wish to record their dissent from the Commission's pronouncements on "segregation," especially as these pronouncements are related to education in the South. Arthur H. Compton, Douglas S. Freeman, Lewis W. Jones, Goodrich C. White. A fuller statement, indicating briefly the basis for this dissent, will appear in volume II of the Commission's report.

and thus the Commission has a tangible figure with which to make its projections.

The Commission believes that in 1960 a minimum of 4,600,000 young people should be enrolled in nonprofit institutions for education beyond the traditional twelfth grade. Of this total number, 2,500,000 should be in the thirteenth and fourteenth grades (junior college level); 1,500,000 in the fifteenth and sixteenth grades (senior college level); and 600,000 in graduate and professional schools beyond the first degree.

In thus appraising future enrollment in institutions of post–high school education, this Commission has not sought to project the future on the basis of the past nor to predict annual enrollments over the period 1948 to 1960. It frankly recognizes that such a forecast would be subject to unpredictable world-wide social and economic conditions.

Appraisal of Talent

The Commission, instead, has staked out what it believes to be the desirable goal in terms of the number of young people that higher education should serve. In so doing it is expressing faith that the American people will invest in the youth of this Nation whatever full educational opportunity may cost. It is expressing, also, confidence that institutions of higher education will make whatever adjustments are required by the increased enrollments. These changes call for educational institutions sufficiently broad in scope and with character variable enough to serve all young people who may reasonably be expected to benefit both themselves and the Nation by further study.

In arriving at the enrollment recommended for 1960, this Commission gave consideration to the results of the Army General Classification Test: the one test of mental ability that had been given to a large and representative group. During World War II almost 10,000,000 men entering the enlisted Army through induction centers took this test.

Three groups were not included among the 10,000,000: those not inducted because of their illiteracy, those inducted as officers and those deferred because they were "engaged in an essential activity." It is assumed that those rejected for physical disabilities would have been distributed over the range of achievement in approximately the same proportions as those inducted into the Army.

Navy personnel are not included. Although data for that group were made available to the Commission, so large a proportion of the Navy were volunteers that Navy figures are less representative of the general population than those of the Army. The Navy included a higher percentage of high school graduates than either the Army or the general population. Hence, the exclusion of Navy data tends to make the conclusions drawn from Army figures conservative.

It may be assumed that the distribution of ability among women is approximately the same as among men. In fact, such AGCT scores as are available for comparison show no significant differences between the two sexes. Furthermore, although the 10,000,000 men given the AGCT were in a relatively restricted age group, there is no reason to believe that the distribution of mental ability would be significantly different between various age groups.

Study of the probable numbers in the excluded groups which would have a depressing effect on the level of the Army's test scores, together with the numbers which would tend to raise the level, indicates, that for mental ability the 10,000,000 men for whom we have AGCT results are conservatively representative of the general population.

The test data gave the distribution of AGCT scores for military personnel by the highest year of schooling each individual had completed at the time of induction; for example, twelfth grade, fourteenth grade. It was thus possible to determine the lowest typical AGCT score of those who had completed a given grade of schooling. There were many individuals with less formal schooling who scored as high or higher than the lowest typical score for a given grade. It follows that those individuals have a reasonable expectation of completing that grade. This consequence is the basis for the Commission's estimate of the proportion of the total population with reasonable expectancies of completing an education at specific levels beyond the high school.

It is true that the AGCT does not measure innate mental ability alone; all such tests, to some degree, indicate educational influences. Educational attainment is related to economic status, to the availability of schools, and to other factors which make for variation in individual educational opportunity. If, hence, there had been greater equality of educational opportunity, the proportion of individuals scoring at or above the critical or lowest typical score for, say high school or 2 or more years of college, would have been higher than the proportion estimated by the Commission.

The AGCT has been equated to various other widely used tests. The most important of these is the American Council on Education Psychological Examination — 1942 College Edition. ACE psychological tests are administered to entering students by several hundred colleges. In estimating "reasonable expectation" of completing the sixteenth school year, equivalent to college graduation, this Commission took for its base an AGCT score equivalent to the twenty-first percentile of the ACE test; thus, only those who would have scored on the ACE test as high as the upper 79 percent of the group admitted to colleges in 1942 have been counted as having a "reasonable expectation" of completing college.

"Reasonable expectation" of completing the 14th school year was based on a minimum AGCT score equivalent to the seventh percentile on the same ACE test. Those who would have scored in the upper 93 percent of the group admitted to college in 1942 were thus included.

National Inventory of Talent

Upon these considerations, this Commission bases what it believes to be conservative estimates of the proportions of the population with reasonable expectations of completing higher education at specific levels. These proportions which constitute this Commission's "National Inventory of Talent" are:

1. At least 49 percent of our population has the mental ability to complete 14 years of schooling with a curriculum of general and vocational studies that should lead either to gainful employment or to further study at a more advanced level.

2. At least 32 percent of our population has the mental ability to complete an advanced liberal or specialized professional education.

If these proportions of American youth are to be admitted to institutions of higher education, we shall have to provide a much greater variety of institutions and programs than we now have to meet their needs. But the Commission has no way of estimating what effect such modifications of the existing system might have on the number of students to be expected.

The probable shift in social attitudes toward the desirability of increased education, together with economic aid, will lead more people to complete additional years of schooling. These factors would undoubtedly increase the proportions in the "inventory," making the estimates not only conservative but probably minimal.

The specific numbers in the "inventory" (see table 8) were computed on the basis of the expected number in the usual age for attendance at junior and senior college levels. These are persons 18–19 years and 20–21 years of age, respectively. The projected enrollments under the "inventory" for graduate and professional schools, above the sixteenth year of schooling, are based on appraisal of the needs of society for people with such training. Estimates of graduate and professional enrollment reflect this Commission's recommendation on making such education increasingly available. For purposes of estimation, all people in school above the sixteenth grade are considered to be at least 22 years of age.

These estimates may be compared with those of the National Resources Development Report which in 1943 suggested that 90 percent of the youth of appropriate ages should attend high school and 80 percent should graduate.

These enrollments proposed for the various levels of higher education probably do not represent the maximum number of students to be expected. There was a tremendous increase in the number and rate of births during and just after World War II. It was thought at first that this was a wartime phenomenon, but the National Office of Vital Statistics now estimates that it will continue at least through 1947. The number of persons born during the period 1943–46, who will be 14–17 years of age in 1960, is reported by the National Office of Vital Statistics to be 877,000 larger than the number born during the period 1939–42, who will be 18–21 years of age in 1960. There is, therefore, every reason to expect that the population in age group 18–21 will continue to increase after 1960 for at least 4 or 5 years, and that there will therefore be a proportionate demand on institutions of higher education.

Table 7 gives the estimates of college age population in 1952 and 1960, and here 1952 is shown only as a point of interest.

TABLE 7 — *Estimate of College Age Population: 1952, 1960**

Age	Population 1952	1960
18–19 years of age	4,099,000	5,104,000
20–21 years of age	4,328,000	4,595,000
Total 18–21 years of age	8,427,000	9,699,000

* Source: Unpublished data of the U. S. Bureau of the Census.

This Commission estimates the specific numbers who should receive higher education in 1952 and 1960 in table 8.

These numbers should be viewed in

produce. Obviously then what this Commission recommends is simply an acceleration of trends in higher education as they were before World War II.

This recommendation is an extension also of the constant trend in American democracy to push ever upward the level of education of our people. As the number completing elementary school increased until it included most of America's children, the opportunity for free public education was extended through the high school. At the present time the increase in the number of youth who complete high school provides the opportunity and creates the necessity for extending public education upward again, at least through the thirteenth and fourteenth year.

It is with respect to enrollments in graduate and professional schools that this Commission's recommendations would lead to a major increase — about 170 percent. This increase reflects the increasing need of the Nation for citizens with such graduate and professional training.

TABLE 8 — *National Inventory of Talent Goals for College Enrollment*

	Inventory of national talent	Goals for college enrollment 1952	1960
13th and 14th grades	49 percent of appropriate age group	2,000,000	2,500,000
15th and 16th grades	32 percent of appropriate age group	1,385,000	1,500,000
Above 16th grade	Based on estimated national need	500,000	600,000
Total		3,885,000	4,600,000

the perspective of their history. The projection of enrollment trends as they existed prior to World War II gives a possible enrollment of 2,924,000 in 1960. Of these 2,704,000 would be in the thirteenth through sixteenth grades, and 220,000 would be in the higher levels. This Commission's recommendations would increase the number of undergraduates only by about 50 percent more than the continuation of the prewar trends would

Only those who view this Commission's recommendations in terms of the situation in, say, 1900 would find them startling. In that year the colleges and universities enrolled less than 150,000 undergraduates, while the estimated potential enrollment was 2,372,000. Year by year these historic potentials were vastly out of proportion to actual enrollments until about 1930. That year the actual enrollment was 30 percent of the potential.

MORE THAN NUMBERS

To provide adequately for this near doubling of the student load in higher education will require a proportionate expansion and improvement of our educational plant, equipment, and personnel.

We may be sure that the private colleges and universities will, in the future as in the past, contribute immeasurably to the expansion and improvement of our facilities for higher education, and it is to be hoped that they will be able to find the necessary funds without increasing the cost to the individual. But in the nature of things, the major burden for equalizing educational opportunity must rest on publicly supported institutions.

Part of the task ahead is to arouse public opinion once more to an awareness of the transcendent importance of education, so that it will not only support but insist on the necessary increase in appropriations for higher education.

To additional community and State support must be added a very considerable measure of Federal assistance. From the Federal Government must come the funds needed to equalize opportunity between region and region, State and State, city and farm. This Federal aid cannot, to serve its purpose, be distributed equally to all; it must be given in proportion to need. The most must go to those who can provide the least for themselves.

Detailed and specific suggestions for financing this desired expansion in our educational enterprise will be made in a later volume of this Commission's report. Here it is necessary only to point out that the United States can afford what it will cost; indeed, we cannot *not* afford it. It is essential to the continued existence of our way of life.

Increase in the numbers to be educated will serve to intensify the problem of devising appropriate and effective programs for higher education. Simply to keep more of our youth in school for a longer period will not of itself, of course, achieve the personal and social ends we have in mind. The measure to which extended educational opportunities accomplish our purposes will depend on the kind of education provided.

As we bring more and more students to the campus, we shall increase in proportion the tremendous variety of human and social needs the college programs must meet. We shall add to the already overwhelming diversity of aptitudes, interests, and levels of attainment that characterize the college student body. And so we shall have to increase the diversification of curricular offerings and of teaching methods and materials to correspond.

Yet in the middle of all the necessary diversity we must somehow preserve and expand a central unity. We must make sure that the education of every student includes the kind of learning and experience that is essential to fit free men to live in a free society.

EDUCATION FOR FREE MEN

American colleges and universities have assumed a huge task in the last half century. To have opened their doors for so many of our youth was difficult enough; to have done so at a time when the complexity of society was increasing rapidly and its pattern was shifting, so that the ends of education itself were subject to continual revision, was to attempt the nearly impossible. The wonder is, not that the colleges have fallen short in some respects, but that they have achieved so considerable a degree of success.

This is no cause for complacency, however. If still greater expansion in number of students is to be undertaken in a period of still greater uncertainty, higher education must act quickly to bring its policies and programs more closely into line with the social purposes it professes to serve.

THE NEED FOR GENERAL EDUCATION

Present college programs are not contributing adequately to the quality of students' adult lives either as workers or as citizens. This is true in large part because the unity of liberal education has been splintered by overspecialization.

For half a century and more the curriculum of the liberal arts college has been expanding and disintegrating to an astounding degree. The number of courses has so multiplied that no student could take all of them, or even a majority of them, in a lifetime. In one small midwestern college, for example, the number of courses offered increased from 67 in 1900 to 296 in 1930. During the same period the liberal arts college of one of the great private universities lengthened its list of courses from 960 to 1,897.

This tendency to diversify the content of what was once an integrated liberal education is in part the consequence of the expansion of the boundaries of knowledge. New advances in every direction have added more and more subjects to the liberal arts curriculum and have at the same time limited the area of knowledge a single course could cover. This development is at once the parent and the child of specialization.

Specialization is a hallmark of our society, and its advantages to mankind have been remarkable. But in the educational program it has become a source both of strength and of weakness. Filtering downward from the graduate and professional school levels, it has taken over the undergraduate years, too, and in the more extreme instances it has made

of the liberal arts college little more than another vocational school, in which the aim of teaching is almost exclusively preparation for advanced study in one or another specialty.

This tendency has been fostered, if not produced, by the training of college teachers in the graduate school, where they are imbued with the single ideal of an ever-narrowing specialism.

The trend toward specialization has been reenforced by the movement toward democratization of higher education. The young people appearing in growing numbers on college campuses have brought with them widely diverse purposes, interests, capacities, and academic backgrounds. Some expect to enter one of the old-line professions; others want training in one of the numerous branches of agriculture, industry or commerce. Some consider college education a natural sequel to high school; others seek it as a road to higher social status.

The net result of the situation is that the college student is faced with a bewildering array of intensive courses from which to make up his individual program. To secure a reasonably comprehensive grasp of his major field, he must in some cases spend as much as half or more of his time in that one department. The other half he scatters among courses in other departments which, designed for future specialists in those fields, are so restricted in scope that the student can gain from them only a fragmentary view of the subject. He, therefore, leaves college unacquainted with some of the fundamental areas of human knowledge and without the integrated view of human experience that is essential both for personal balance and for social wisdom.

Today's college graduate may have gained technical or professional training in one field of work or another,

but is only incidentally, if at all, made ready for performing his duties as a man, a parent, and a citizen. Too often he is "educated" in that he has acquired competence in some particular occupation, yet falls short of that human wholeness and civic conscience which the cooperative activities of citizenship require.

The failure to provide any core of unity in the essential diversity of higher education is a cause for grave concern. A society whose members lack a body of common experience and common knowledge is a society without a fundamental culture; it tends to disintegrate into a mere aggregation of individuals. Some community of values, ideas, and attitudes is essential as a cohesive force in this age of minute division of labor and intense conflict of special interests.

The crucial task of higher education today, therefore, is to provide a unified general education for American youth. Colleges must find the right relationship between specialized training on the one hand, aiming at a thousand different careers, and the transmission of a common cultural heritage toward a common citizenship on the other.

There have already been many efforts to define this relationship. Attempts to reach conclusions about the ends and means of general education have been a major part of debate and experimentation in higher education for at least two decades.

"General education" is the term that has come to be accepted for those phases of nonspecialized and nonvocational learning which should be the common experience of all educated men and women.

General education should give to the student the values, attitudes, knowledge, and skills that will equip him to live

rightly and well in a free society. It should enable him to identify, interpret, select, and build into his own life those components of his cultural heritage that contribute richly to understanding and appreciation of the world in which he lives. It should therefore embrace ethical values, scientific generalizations, and aesthetic conceptions, as well as an understanding of the purposes and character of the political, economic and social institutions that men have devised.

But the knowledge and understanding which general education aims to secure whether drawn from the past or from a living present, are not to be regarded as ends in themselves. They are means to a more abundant personal life and a stronger, freer social order.

Thus conceived, general education is not sharply distinguished from liberal education; the two differ mainly in degree, not in kind. General education undertakes to redefine liberal education in terms of life's problems as men face them, to give it human orientation and social direction, to invest it with content that is directly relevant to the demands of contemporary society. General education is liberal education with its matter and method shifted from its original aristocratic intent to the service of democracy. General education seeks to extend to all men the benefits of an education that liberates.

This purpose calls for a unity in the program of studies that a uniform system of courses cannot supply. The unity must come, instead, from a consistency of aim that will infuse and harmonize all teaching and all campus activities.

OBJECTIVES OF GENERAL EDUCATION

The purposes of general education should be understood in terms of performance, of behavior, not in terms of mastering particular bodies of knowledge. It is the task of general education to provide the kinds of learning and experience that will enable the student to attain certain basic outcomes, among them the following:

1. To develop for the regulation of one's personal and civic life a code of behavior based on ethical principles consistent with democratic ideals.

Many colleges have tended in recent decades to concern themselves with the intellect alone. They have left to other agencies or to chance the student's spiritual and ethical development.

But they obviously cannot leave the whole field of individual purpose, discipline, character, and values to the accidents of environment before and after college. Students should be stimulated and aided to define their personal and social purposes in life. Personal integrity and consistent behavior are impossible where such conscious purpose is lacking.

General education can foster and quicken respect for ideals and values. Wise men, of course, have never doubted the importance of ethical considerations, but for a generation or two these matters seem to have been out of fashion among sophisticated intellectuals. If anything is clear in these troubled times, it is the urgent need of soundly based ideals to guide personal and social relationships in a world where insecurity is steadily weakening trust between man and man.

Interpersonal relations, business relations, labor relations, even international relations, depend, if they are to prosper, on good faith, decent intentions, and mutual confidence. Suspicion of the other fellow's motives and fear that he will not play the game according to the rules are far too prevalent for either individual or national health.

Such a condition is appropriate to a Fascist state, which rests on the rule that no one can trust anyone else; it has no place in a democratic society. To cooperate for common ends, we must have faith in each other.

Ethical principles that will induce this faith need not be based on any single sanction or be authoritarian in origin, nor need finality be claimed for them. Some persons will find the satisfactory basis for a moral code in the democratic creed itself, some in philosophy, some in religion. Religion is held to be a major force in creating the system of human values on which democracy is predicated, and many derive from one or another of its varieties a deepened sense of human worth and a strengthened concern for the rights of others.

2. To participate actively as an informed and responsible citizen in solving the social, economic, and political problems of one's community, State, and Nation.

3. To recognize the interdependence of the different peoples of the world and one's personal responsibility for fostering international understanding and peace.

The urgency of these two objectives and the necessity for heightening the sense of social responsibility they call for have already been pointed out in Chapter II. The extent to which present educational programs are failing to serve these ends is a measure of the importance they must assume in general education in the immediate future.

As a rule the graduates of our schools and colleges have not been adequately prepared for the tasks of citizenship and have been apathetic about performing them. Not only general observation but statistical studies of the attitudes and activities of college graduates have revealed the low level of their civic knowledge and their participation in social action. Many of them were not only uninformed about national and world problems but were markedly reluctant to take part in social enterprises at any cost to themselves. For most of them, direct political activity was limited to marking the ballot on election day, and not all of them bothered to do even that.

We dare not let this state of affairs continue. Every resource of education must be mobilized and focused on the task of establishing in students a habit of social action enlightened by insight into the responsibilities of citizenship at all levels — local, national, and international. Recognition of social planning as a new tool which advances the methods of gathering and appraising information in the hands of democratic society is one of the concepts which general education should seek to make clear to students.

To teach the meaning and the processes of democracy, the college campus itself should be employed as a laboratory of the democratic way of life. Ideas and ideals become dynamic as they are lived, and the habit of cooperation in a common enterprise can be gained most surely in practice. But this learning cannot take place in institutions of higher education that are operated on authoritarian principles.

The varied activities of the campus provide many avenues through which students could participate in making decisions and share in carrying forward their joint undertaking. If the college were conducted as a community rather than as a hotel, it would afford much greater opportunity for students to acquire the practical experience so essential to the life of democracy outside the college.

Nor should the college neglect the educational resources in that life "outside." Including "field experience"—work, travel, research, and study projects in the community off-campus — as part of the program of general education can do much to break down the present tendency toward isolation of the college from the wider community in which the student is to live after college.

4. To understand the common phenomena in one's physical environment, to apply habits of scientific thought to both personal and civic problems, and to appreciate the implications of scientific discoveries for human welfare.

The scientific account of the natural world must, of course, hold a prominent place in the school experience of all educated persons. To simplify this account and give it relevance for the life and problems of ordinary men is one of the most important and at the same time most difficult objectives of general education.

A just criticism of most courses in natural science is that they are confined to some special field such as physics, chemistry, or zoology, and that most of the study in them is directed toward preparing future scientists and not toward educating future citizens. What is needed instead is the integration of the significant methods and findings of the natural sciences into a comprehensive synthesis that will bring to the general student understanding of the fundamental nature of the physical world in which he lives and of the skills by which this nature is discerned.

That the student grasp the processes involved in scientific thought and understand the principles of scientific method is even more important than that he should know the data of the sciences. The spirit of science — including intellectual curiosity, openness of mind, passion for truth wherever it may lead, respect for evidence, and the free communication of discoveries — should be the product of education at all levels.

General education in science must also emphasize the social significance of science and technology for our times. Failure to understand how science has transformed the conditions under which men live is failure to understand the forces that have reshaped our civilization and now threaten to destroy it. At this of all times it should be clear that understanding the social implications of the sciences is an imperative in general education.

5. To understand the ideas of others and to express one's own effectively.

Developing the skills of communication is perhaps the least debatable of the objectives of general education. Without free, clear, and distinct communication a true meeting of minds does not occur, and understanding and cooperation are retarded if not prevented. And to communicate easily and well with one's fellows one must be able to write and to read, to talk and to listen.

Experience indicates the close relationship that exists between thought and the symbols that express thought. Clear and precise thinking requires good language habits. Few of the abilities men possess are of greater human significance than their power to order ideas clearly and to set these before their fellows by tongue or pen.

The ability to read — not merely to call words and pronounce symbols but really to grasp the meaning and follow the logic of the writer — is basic to all other human enterprises. To say that the youth in our schools and colleges should learn how to read may seem to be repeating the obvious, but scientific studies have revealed the low level of literacy attained by a large part of our adult population. The experience of college teachers affirms that many students enter the colleges, and not a few graduate, without having acquired more than an elementary degree of practical skill in reading. This skill is a primary objective of general education.

Numbers are also an important means of communication. We call mathematics into service in our daily lives much more frequently than is generally supposed. General education must provide a functional knowledge of the elements of mathematics that industrial society normally requires, and also the skill of quantitative thinking.

6. To attain a satisfactory emotional and social adjustment.

General education does not stop with the development of intellectual powers. For a satisfying and successful life a person must also be emotionally stable and mature, able to endure the conflicts and tensions, the compromises and defeats, that life is almost certain to bring. He must develop the strength of mind and heart to stand alone if necessary, when his sense of justice and good conscience compel him to an unpopular course of action.

As a rule, however, a man's happiness and his achievement will depend in considerable measure upon his capacity for association with others. And this turns more upon personality traits than upon intellectual powers. It is all too often the case that a man is unable to make the most of his abilities because he cannot get on well with people or cannot find his way around easily in the maze of social custom and organization.

American schools and colleges have hitherto paid little attention to the educational implications of this fact. They have been so preoccupied with the training of the intellect, with making sure students could pass examinations in sizable bodies of knowledge of this or that, that they have given little consideration to the problems of personality. General education should correct this deficiency. It should make growth in emotional and social adjustment one of its major aims.

To this end, the student should be taught the nature of human behavior, his own and others'; he should understand the highly important role of emotions in our lives; he should have guidance and practice in applying this knowledge in his own adjustment to men and life. Instruction in psychology and the social sciences can provide the knowledge he needs, and experience in the wide range of activities afforded by the college community can provide the field for its application and testing.

7. To maintain and improve his own health and to cooperate actively and intelligently in solving community health problems.

In any society human resources are of paramount importance, and when the physical health and vitality of any large proportion of the people are less than they might be, these resources are seriously impaired. The mental vigor and spirit of a people are conditioned by its state of physical health.

Our colleges and universities are doing far less than they might to dispel the ignorance that lies at the root of the ill health of many of our people. Almost all our colleges, it is true, offer many courses that touch in some degree on the principles and practices of healthful living. But these courses are scattered through a number of departments, and the information contained in them is never brought directly to bear on the practical problems of personal and community health.

What is needed is a course that deals specifically and explicitly with the information, attitudes, and habits the student needs to maintain and improve his own health and that of his community. An important phase of instruction to this end will be emphasis on the fact that health is more than a personal problem, that it has social implications, and that the individual owes it to society no less than to himself to keep his health and energy at their peak.

College programs of physical education should provide an opportunity for the student to put into practice his theoretical knowledge of healthful habits. But to serve this purpose, most such programs need reorientation. They should concentrate on the activities that the average person can carry on into life after college, rather than on the training of a few athletes for intercollegiate competition or on the technical preparation of those who plan to make a profession of physical education. The emotional value of participation in "spectator sports" is not to be discounted, but it needs to be balanced by more direct personal activity than is engaged in by most college graduates.

8. To understand and enjoy literature, art, music, and other cultural activities as expressions of personal and social experience, and to participate to some extent in some form of creative activity.

It can scarcely be necessary to urge the importance of literature in the program of general education. Man's consuming interest is in man, and in this interest literature can serve. By means of great novels, poems, plays, and essays one can participate vicariously in many events that one's own life does not encompass, and so can gain as in no other way imaginative insight into the emotions, drives, and aspirations of one's fellow men.

Literature sets forth both the heights

43920

and the depths that man can reach. It is an avenue of communication with the great minds and the great souls of yesterday and of today. It can do as much as any other single form of experience to broaden and deepen the perceptions and sympathies of the individual.

This consequence does not, however, follow from the study of details of literary history, literary biography, literary techniques, or any other of the accompaniments to literature that make up specialization in the subject. The contribution of literature to insight and emotional maturity will come from one's own reading of the world's literary treasures, and from reflection upon them.

The world's literary treasures are not those of the West alone. They include the great intellectual statements of men everywhere and in all ages. There is probably no better way of promoting the intellectual and spiritual unity of mankind than through free trade in enduring literary expressions.

And in the graphic and plastic arts, too, man has recorded much of his thought and feeling about life through color, form, and sound. A signal defect in much of American education, and in American culture, is its failure to recognize that music, painting, sculpture, the dance, the drama, and others of the arts are authentic statements of experience.

One of the tasks of American democracy is to heighten and diffuse esthetic sensibility and good taste, to make our people sensitive to beauty in all its varied forms: in the commodities and services of everyday life, in private and public buildings, in community and regional planning.

The study of the arts in general education should not be directed toward the development of creative artists of exceptional gifts, though it may in some instances lead to this. It should aim at appreciation of the arts as forms of human expression, at awakening or intensifying the student's sensitivity to beauty and his desire to create beauty in his everyday surroundings, at developing bases for discrimination and interpretation, at inducing sympathy with arts and artists and active concern for their welfare. Support of the arts can no longer be left to the patronage of wealth; active encouragement of artistic expression in its various forms must become the responsibility of all citizens.

Before completing his general education, the student should acquire a measure of skill in at least one of the arts or crafts, in some form of musical expression or in dramatics. Participation in creative activity, even at a low level of proficiency, is one of the best means to understanding and appreciation of artistic expression.

9. To acquire the knowledge and attitudes basic to a satisfying family life.

In spite of the fundamental role our culture assigns to marriage and the family, in spite of their encompassing importance for a happy personal life, higher education has in the past concerned itself little with preparing students for their roles as mates and as parents. Here again, pertinent facts and materials have been scattered in bits through the curriculum but until very recently little attempt has been made to integrate them and focus them on the problem as it affects the average person in his everyday life. Courses in "The Family" have been set up for the sociologist, anthropologist, or social worker, but not to meet the needs of the general student.

Such a general course would include, as a minimum, psychological preparation for the emotional adjustments normally called for in marriage; child care and training; the planning of the home, of the physical environment of the family; consumer education in budgeting the family income, in wise buying and spending; and the principles of nutrition, for the proper feeding of the family. None of these matters are new to the college curriculum; only bringing them together in courses focused on the problems of family life is new.

That success in marriage and child rearing does not follow automatically from competence in other spheres is abundantly evident from the broken marriages, broken homes, and maladjusted children that are becoming all too common in America. Education for emotional stability, and probably for social competence and democratic living too, must begin in early childhood. Children reared in a home atmosphere of emotional insecurity, of social isolation, and of authoritarian discipline will not respond readily to education toward other ends in school and college.

General education will render a real service to our society as well as to individual students if it makes preparation for a stable, happy, all-sharing family life one of its primary concerns.

10. To choose a socially useful and personally satisfying vocation that will permit one to use to the full his particular interests and abilities.

Although direct vocational training is not a part of general education, occupational orientation should be. Few things make more difference in the quality of one's life, in one's vigor, good heart, and joy in living, than satisfaction in one's daily work. Fortunate above all others is the man whose way of earning a living is for him also an effective means of self-realization and self-expression. But this happy state seems to be the exception; more often the individual feels a sharp distinction between his earning hours and his living hours.

Satisfactory vocational adjustment might occur more often if there were less occupational snobbery among us, if all forms of useful work were accorded equal social status — manual labor as well as the white-collar job, mechanical skills as well as verbal aptitudes. Through education society should come to recognize the equal dignity of all kinds of work, and so erase distinctions based on occupational caste.

General education should acquaint the student with the interdependence among jobs that characterizes the world at work. It should also make clear the close relationship that exists between one's abilities and interests and his satisfaction in a given line of work. The student should be helped to choose his vocation on a more objective and sensible basis than the ambitions of his parents, his own wishful thinking, or incomplete occupational information.

It is experience on the job that best permits the student to measure theory against practice and to learn what abilities and skills his chosen work will require of him. Some colleges, such as Antioch and Bennington and Black Mountain, have found off-campus work, alternated with periods of study, a fruitful method of helping students to see the relevance of their college courses and to discover their own talents and occupational disposition.

11. To acquire and use the skills and habits involved in critical and constructive thinking.

Ability to think and to reason, within the limits set by one's mental capacity, should be the distinguishing mark of an educated person. The conception long prevailed in our Western tradition that Latin and Greek, mathematics, and formal logic were the most effective instruments for developing the power to think. These disciplines can be made to contribute richly to that end, but so can many others. Development of the reasoning faculty, of the habit of critical appraisal, should be the constant and pervasive aim of all education, in every field and at every level.

Higher education has sometimes seemed to proceed on the assumption that the student can acquire in college all the information about all the subjects he may need to know and use in later years. It has stressed the absorption of as many facts about as many things as possible.

More to the purpose and of much more lasting effect would be emphasis on the student's acquiring familiarity with the processes of inquiry and discovery. Insofar as education is not indoctrination it is discovery, and discovery is the product of inquiry. Arousing and stimulating intellectual curiosity, channeling this curiosity into active and comprehensive investigation, and developing skill in gathering, analyzing, and evaluating evidence — these should constitute the primary job of every teacher from the elementary grades through the university. The open and inquiring mind and the habit of rigorous and disciplined investigation are the marks of freemen and the sinews of a free society.

General education, therefore, will concentrate, not on the mastery of specific information, but on the fullest possible development of the motives, attitudes, and habits that will enable the student to inform himself and think for himself throughout life. It will stress (1) the importance of being informed, of basing decisions, actions, and opinions on accurate facts; (2) knowledge of where and how to acquire information; (3) ability to appraise, relate, and integrate facts in order to form valid judgments. The habit of making this approach to any situation can best be developed by leading the student to apply it at every opportunity in his life on the campus, in solving problems both inside and outside the classroom. . . .

EDUCATION ADJUSTED TO NEEDS

To make sure of its own health and strength a democratic society must provide free and equal access to education for its youth, and at the same time it must recognize their differences in capacity and purpose. Higher education in America should include a variety of institutional forms and educational programs, so that at whatever point any student leaves school, he will be fitted, within the limits of his mental capacity and educational level, for an abundant and productive life as a person, as a worker, and as a citizen.

THE COMMUNITY COLLEGE

As one means of achieving the expansion of educational opportunity and the diversification of educational offerings it considers necessary, this Commission recommends that the number of community colleges be increased and that their activities be multiplied.

Community colleges in the future may be either publicly or privately controlled and supported, but most of them, obviously, will be under public auspices. They will be mainly local or regional in scope and should be locally controlled, though they should be carefully planned to fit into a comprehensive State-wide system of higher education. They will derive much of their support from the local community, supplemented by aid from State funds.

Some community colleges may offer a full four years of college work, but most of them probably will stop at the end of the fourteenth grade, the sophomore year of the traditional college. In the latter case they should be closely articulated with the high school.

Whatever form the community college takes, its purpose is educational service to the entire community, and this purpose requires of it a variety of functions and programs. It will provide college education for the youth of the community certainly, so as to remove geographic and economic barriers to educational opportunity and discover and develop individual talents at low cost and easy access. But in addition, the community college will serve as an active center of adult education. It will attempt to meet the total post–high school needs of its community.

Terminal and Semiprofessional Education

In the past the junior college has most commonly sought to provide within the local community the freshman and sophomore courses of the traditional college curriculum. With notable exceptions, it has concentrated on preparing students for further study in the junior and senior years of liberal arts colleges or professional schools.

But preparatory programs looking to the more advanced courses of the senior college are not complete and rounded in themselves, and they usually do not serve well the purpose of those who must terminate their schooling at the end of the fourteenth grade. Half the young people who go to college find themselves unable to complete the full 4-year course, and for a long time to come more students will end their formal education in the junior college years than will prolong it into the senior college. These 2-year

graduates would gain more from a terminal program planned specifically to meet their needs than from the first half of a 4-year curriculum.

For this reason, the Commission recommends that the community college emphasize programs of terminal education.

These terminal programs should include both general education and vocational training. They should be designed both for young people who want to secure as good a general education as possible by the end of the fourteenth grade and for those who wish to fit themselves for semiprofessional occupations.

Semiprofessional training, properly conceived and organized, can make a significant contribution to education for society's occupational requirements. In not providing this sort of training anywhere in existing programs, the educational system is out of step with the demands of the twentieth century American economy.

Because of advancing technology, the occupational center of our economic system is shifting away from the major producing industries. The proportion of the working population engaged in these industries has decreased, while the proportion in the distributive and service trades has increased. In 1880, for instance, about one-half of all workers were engaged in agriculture; in 1947, less than one-seventh of the workers were so engaged.

One result of this development is a new and rapidly growing need for trained semiprofessional workers in these distributive and service occupations. To meet the needs of the economy our schools must train many more young people for employment as medical secretaries, recreational leaders, hotel and restaurant managers, aviators, salesmen in fields like life insurance and real estate, photographers, automotive and electrical technicians, and so on through a long list of positions in the business and professional world.

Education on the technician level — that is, the training of medical technicians, dental hygienists, nurses' aides, laboratory technicians — offers one practical solution for the acute shortage of professional personnel in medicine, dentistry, and nursing. An adequate staff of well-trained assistants can substantially increase the number of patients one doctor, dentist, or nurse can handle.

For these semiprofessional occupations a full 4 years of college training is not necessary. It is estimated that in many fields of work there are *five* jobs requiring 2 years of college preparation for every *one* that requires 4 years. Training for these more numerous jobs is the kind the community college should provide.

If the semiprofessional curriculum is to accomplish its purpose, however, it must not be crowded with vocational and technical courses to the exclusion of general education. It must aim at developing a combination of social understanding and technical competence. Semiprofessional education should mix a goodly amount of general education for personal and social development with technical education that is intensive, accurate, and comprehensive enough to give the student command of marketable abilities.

Community Center of Learning

Post–high school education for youth is only one of the functions to be performed by the community college. One such college has been known to have a daytime junior college enrollment of 3,000 but an adult enrollment in the late afternoon and evening of 25,000.

The community college seeks to become a center of learning for the entire community, with or without the restrictions that surround formal course work in traditional institutions of higher education. It gears its programs and services to the needs and wishes of the people it serves, and its offerings may range from workshops in painting or singing or play writing for fun to refresher courses in journalism or child psychology.

If the health of the community can be improved by teaching restaurant managers something about the bacteriology of food, the community college sets up such a course and seeks to enroll as many of those employed in food service as it can muster. If the community happens to be a center for travelers from Latin America, the college provides classes in Spanish for salespeople, waitresses, bellboys, and taxicab drivers.

The potential effects of the community college in keeping intellectual curiosity alive in out-of-school citizens, of stimulating their zest for learning, of improving the quality of their lives as individuals and as citizens are limited only by the vision, the energy, and the ingenuity of the college staff — and by the size of the college budget. But the people will take care of the budget if the staff provides them with vital and worthwhile educational services.

In Relation to the Liberal Arts College

The Commission does not intend to suggest that the expansion of educational opportunity at the freshman-sophomore level should be limited to the community college. Part of the needed expansion can be achieved through existing 4-year colleges, part of it through the lower divisions of the universities.

Some of the established colleges may wish to institute terminal curriculums and contribute to the development of semiprofessional training. Others will prefer to concentrate on general education for students who plan to complete a 4-year course. Still others, especially the liberal arts colleges of universities, may welcome the opportunity to focus their energies on senior college programs.

In any case, the liberal arts college is so well established in the American educational tradition that it need not fear community colleges will weaken its own appeal. It should encourage the development of the community college, not oppose it. Experience indicates that these community institutions awaken intellectual curiosity and ambition in many youth who would not otherwise seek college education at all, and in many cases these students will be stimulated to continue their college careers if the 4-year colleges will meet them halfway with liberal admission policies.

There is little danger of lowered standards in this. We know now that ability to complete successfully the work of the last 2 years of college depends more upon the quality of mind and the mental habits a student brings to his work than upon the nature of the subject matter he has already covered. There is no reason to believe that community colleges, if they are adequately staffed, cannot do as good a job as the lower divisions of 4-year colleges in preparing students for advanced work in liberal and professional education.

While it favors the growth of community colleges, the Commission emphasizes that they must be soundly established with respect to financial support and student attendance. This calls for careful planning on a State-wide basis in determining location of the colleges and the curriculums to be offered. Simply to create more small, inadequately financed institutions would only retard the develop-ment **of a sound program of post—high school education. . . .**

THE SOCIAL ROLE OF HIGHER EDUCATION

The task that President Truman assigned to this Commission was to define the responsibilities of higher education in American democracy and in international affairs, and to reexamine the objectives, methods, and facilities of higher education in the light of the social role it has to play.

In the first volume of its report, this Commission has declared its conviction that if American higher education is to fulfill its responsibilities in the second half of the twentieth century, it will have to accelerate its adjustment in purpose, scope, content, and organization to the crucial needs of our time. It will have to act quickly and boldly if it is to fit students for meeting the new problems and necessities America faces as the Nation takes on a responsibility for world leadership that is without parallel in history.

American colleges and universities must envision a much larger role for higher education in the national life. They can no longer consider themselves merely the instrument for producing an intellectual elite; they must become the means by which every citizen, youth, and adult is enabled and encouraged to carry his education, formal and informal, as far as his native capacities permit.

This conception is the inevitable consequence of the democratic faith; universal education is indispensable to the full and living realization of the democratic ideal. No society can long remain free unless its members are freemen, and men are not free where ignorance prevails. No more in mind than in body can this

Nation or any endure half slave, half free. Education that liberates and ennobles must be made equally available to all. Justice to the individual demands this; the safety and progress of the Nation depend upon it. America cannot afford to let any of its potential human resources go undiscovered and undeveloped.

E PLURIBUS UNUM

The wider diffusion of more education, however, will not serve the purpose unless that education is better adapted to contemporary needs. The first and most essential charge upon higher education is that at all its levels and in all its fields of specialization it shall be the carrier of democratic values, ideals, and processes.

Democracy as a way of life uses varied institutional forms and changing patterns of cooperative association as time and circumstances may require, but it holds fast to its abiding elements: Its respect for human personality, its insistence on the fullest freedom of belief and expression for all citizens, its principle that all should participate in decisions that concern themselves, its faith in reason, its deep obligation to promote human well-being. These ideals and the processes through which they are translated into individual and social behavior must permeate American education from the nursery school through the highest reaches of the graduate and professional schools.

It is imperative that American education develop a "democratic dynamic" that will inspire faith in the democratic way of life, dispel doubt and defeatism about the future, and imbue youth with the conviction that life has high purpose and that they are active and responsible participants in that purpose.

At the same time and with equal urgency higher education must prepare Americans to contribute their utmost to the achievement of world order and peace among men. To this end it should seek to inculcate in students a sympathetic understanding of the cultures and peoples that make up the world community. Higher education faces no greater challenge than that of securing, and securing in time, a widespread recognition of and adjustment to the oneness of the modern world. The task of the colleges here is to make the transition from a curriculum centered almost exclusively on the American–West European tradition to one that embodies the intellectual experience of the whole of mankind.

E Pluribus Unum — From many persons one nation, and from many peoples one world — indivisible, with liberty and justice for all. A strong and dynamic national community, intertwining in harmony and unity of purpose an infinite variety of individual talents and careers, and in time a strong and dynamic world community, embracing in brotherhood and mutual respect a rich and enriching diversity of national cultures. These are the twin goals which America, and therefore its institutions of higher education, must strive to attain.

THE CURRICULUM

Incessant search for new knowledge through research, unceasing effort to plumb the meaning of life and the enigma of man's behavior through interpretive scholarship, the cultivation of gifted minds, the provision of professional education to satisfy the occupational needs of society — these are the established tasks of higher education. They are vital tasks, and their performance must be constantly improved and strengthened. But to them now higher education must add a sufficient variety of organizational arrangements and curricular offerings to encompass the wide range of individual differences in capacity and purpose that increasing the number of students will bring to college.

At the same time there must be sufficient unity of purpose in this essential diversity of higher education to produce a community of values and ideas among educated men. The complexity of modern society requires a great variety of talents and many kinds of competence for its successful functioning; yet without some commonality of purpose, values, and experience we shall not achieve the reconciliation of differing opinions and interests that is the lifeblood of democracy.

FEDERAL AID

The radical character of the adjustments required in higher education, their magnitude, and the pressure of time, all mean that neither individual institutions nor national educational organizations have the resources to effect the necessary changes without outside stimulation and financial assistance. These, the Commission believes, will have to come from the Federal Government.

The particular ways in which Federal support and encouragement should be given will be discussed in later reports. Here, this Commission wishes only to point out that such aid to higher education is a proper concern of the Federal Government, because the health and strength of higher education is a matter of serious national import.

The Federal Government assumes responsibility for supplementing State and local efforts in military defense against the Nation's enemies without; surely it may as justifiably assume responsibility for supplementing State and local efforts

against educational deficiencies and inequalities that are democracy's enemies within.

We may be sure our democracy will not survive unless American schools and colleges are given the means for improvement and expansion. This is a primary call upon the Nation's resources. We dare not disregard it. America's strength at home and abroad in the years ahead will be determined in large measure by the quality and the effectiveness of the education it provides for its citizens. . . .

THE ROLE OF THE FEDERAL GOVERNMENT

The two preceding chapters have presented the expenditures and income of higher education. They have been shown in terms of their past and present relationship; they have been projected to 1960 in terms of the numbers to be served and the kind and quality of higher education which, in the judgment of this Commission, the needs of the nation and its people fully justify.

As the total sources of income are appraised against expenditures, a number of conclusions become evident — conclusions that are extremely important for arriving at sound policies for financing higher education over the years ahead.

1. This Commission believes that the potentialities of income from private sources are such that the annual additional funds needed to maintain a high-quality program of education and research in privately controlled institutions can be obtained if they will maintain their total enrollment at about 900,000 — which is approximately their 1946–47 level. *The belief that the additional funds can be secured rests on the ability of the privately controlled institutions themselves to work out and to adopt appropriate and concerted fund-raising meth-*

ods and appeals. It is the conclusion of the Commission, however, that the additional cost of the expanded program and enrollments for higher education which have been recommended must of necessity be borne by public funds.

2. The elimination of student fees for the thirteenth and fourteenth grades and the reduction in fees above the fourteenth grade in publicly controlled institutions recommended by this Commission, will require that a large part of the income derived presently from such sources be secured from public appropriations.

3. Large amounts of additional funds may be expected from the States with the help of local governments. As repeatedly emphasized in the preceding chapter, the States should continue their present proportion of the cost of colleges and universities and, where their resources permit, substantially increase their appropriations for higher education. *But even with a great increase in effort, as pointed out in Chapter III, the States will not be able alone to meet the expanding needs of the nation for college and university education.*

4. On the basis of these conclusions, and with a continuance of the present federal assistance, exclusive of the funds provided under the GI Bill and other temporary appropriations, it has been shown that to serve 4,600,000 students, additional funds of more than $600,000,000 annually will be required by 1960 for educational and general expenditures — the day-to-day operation of the system of higher education. When the needed expansion in capital outlay is taken into account, the unbalance reaches a figure of far greater proportion.

This unbalance, large and serious as it is, can be eliminated and the budget balanced in 1960 if the American people are willing to value higher edu-cation in its true worth, and provide the financial support which its value both to the individual and to the nation more than justifies. To do so, however, will require that the role of the Federal Government, as a partner with the States in the support of higher education, be greatly strengthened and expanded. That role must be based upon sound principles of Federal-State relationships, carefully planned and geared to the needs and responsibilities of higher education in a democracy....**

BASIC PRINCIPLES OF FEDERAL RELATION-
SHIPS TO HIGHER LEARNING

The relationship of the Federal Government to higher education is of vital concern not only to the colleges and universities, but to the Nation. Neither the earlier assistance based on special interest, nor the emergency appropriations of the depression and of the war periods offer a general pattern for the future.

The time has come for America to develop a sound pattern of continuing Federal support for higher education. The analyses presented in the preceding chapter show that the Federal Government must assume a large and important role in financing higher education.

The following basic principles are those which this Commission believes should guide the development and expansion of Federal financial relationship with higher education.

1. In its relationships to higher education, the Federal Government should recognize the national importance of a well-rounded and well-integrated program of education for all citizens, regardless of age, sex, race, creed, or economic and social status

Hereafter, Federal funds appropriated for education should not be used to promote one phase or level of education at the expense of another. It is in the interest of the national welfare that all levels and phases of education from the nursery school to the post-graduate school be of high quality. This means, therefore, that *Federal support for higher education should presuppose a strong and effective system of elementary and secondary education.*

Federal support for higher education should assist the States and localities to provide equality of educational opportunity for each individual able and willing to receive it.

2. Federal funds for the general support of institutions of higher education should be distributed among the States on an equalization basis

The plan of Federal aid should take proper account of the relative needs of the States for higher education, and of their varying economic abilities to meet these needs. It should provide that all States participate in the allocation of Federal equalization funds, each in proportion to its relative need. *It is important for the Federal Government to give some aid and encouragement in the development and improvement of higher education in the wealthier States, but its primary responsibility is to insure the maintenance of an acceptable minimum program in the poorer States.*

3. Federal appropriations for the general support of higher education should clearly recognize the responsibility of the States for the administration and control of the education programs

Federal funds for the development and general support of higher education should be paid to the States, not directly to the colleges and universities themselves. This procedure is necessary to in-

sure coordination of State programs, and to avoid duplication, overlapping, and dual control by government. Federal assistance should supplement, but never supplant, the maximum effort of each State to carry the cost of its system of higher education. *The role of the Federal Government should be that of a partner with the States in their joint concern for those outcomes of education vital to national interests and to the rights of all American citizens under the Constitution.*

4. Adequate safeguards should be established by the Federal Government to assure the full realization of the purposes for which aid is to be granted

These safeguards should include the requirements of a post-audit and the publication of adequate reports by the States and institutions participating in Federally sponsored programs. They should include authority for the Federal agency administering the law to withhold funds from any State or local agency which fails to meet the prescribed provisions.

Any Federal measure intended to achieve equal opportunity for all American youth should contain provisions to insure, that in sections of the country where separated systems of education are maintained on a basis of race, sufficient regulatory powers are vested in the Federal Government to permit withholding of appropriations whenever it is established that racial or minority groups are being discriminated against by the disbursement of such funds. Full implementation of the recommendations of this Commission for the equalization of educational opportunity for all youth is not possible otherwise.

5. Federal funds for the general support of current educational activities and for general capital outlay

purposes should be appropriated for use only in institutions under public control

A prime responsibility of government in a democracy is to provide equal opportunities for all its citizens to receive a high quality education. This is implied in the "general welfare clause" of the Federal Constitution. It has been recognized by the people of almost every State in the form of specific constitutional mandates to the State legislatures.

To discharge this responsibility, it is thus the fundamental obligation of government to establish a sound system of public education and to support it to the fullest extent possible. It is a denial of this responsibility when at any time the chosen representatives of all the people neglect to meet fully this basic obligation.

The responsibility for providing a strong system of public education does not, however, deny in any way to any individual or group of individuals the right to attend, or to establish and support in addition to public schools, a private or denominational institution for the purpose of providing, within limits prescribed by law, a kind of education which such individuals or groups deem more suitable to their particular needs and beliefs. It is just as undemocratic for the government to restrict in any way this fundamental right, as it is for government to fail to meet its prime responsibility for a strong system of public education. Nevertheless, any diversion by government of public funds to the general support of nonpublicly controlled educational institutions tends to deny the acceptance of the fundamental responsibility and to weaken the program of public education.

Sound public policy demands, furthermore, that State and local public educa- tional bodies be able to exercise at all times the right to review and control educational policies in any institution or agency for which public monies are appropriated and expended. Public responsibility for support of education implies public responsibility for the policies which are supported. It follows, therefore, that the acceptance of public funds by any institution, public or private, should carry with it the acceptance of the right of the people as a whole to exercise review and control of the educational policies and procedures of that institution. Such acceptance by privately controlled institutions would, in the opinion of this Commission, tend to destroy the competitive advantages and free inquiry which they have established and which are so important in providing certain safeguards to freedom. It would be contrary to the best interests of these institutions as well as to those of society in general.

It has long been an established principle in America that the responsibility for education resides with the States. This principle stems from the clause in the Federal Constitution which provides that all functions of government not specifically allocated to the Federal Government by the Constitution shall be left to the States. The Commission believes, therefore, that the determination of what institutions or systems of education are publicly controlled and thus eligible to receive public funds for the support of higher education, as recommended by this Commission, should be left to the States.

6. **Federal funds provided for scholarships or grants-in-aid for the purpose of helping individuals of ability and fellowships for those of special talent to obtain equality**

of opportunity in education should be paid directly to the qualifying individuals

It is in keeping with the principles of democracy that each individual should have as free choice as facilities permit in determining the educational institution which he deems most suitable to his needs and interests, regardless of whether that institution is under public, private, or church control. That choice can be fully protected only if scholarships or fellowships, such as those proposed by this Commission in Volume II, "Equalizing and Expanding Individual Opportunity," are paid directly to the qualifying individuals.

7. **As is deemed necessary, the Federal Government should make contracts with individual institutions, publicly or privately controlled, for specific services authorized by national legislation**

It is in the best interests of the national welfare that the Federal Government be able to contract for services authorized by national legislation with whatever institution or agency can most efficiently and economically provide the kinds of services needed. These services may include projects for research or training. In order to insure the protection of the public interest, such contracts should express explicitly the terms under which the services are to be provided, including the capital outlay essential to conduct them. . . .

A FINAL WORD

In this chapter the President's Commission has recommended the basis for a strong continuing role of the Federal Government in financing higher education. It has proposed a role commensurate with the responsibilities of higher education in a democracy; a role which,

when accepted in full, will make college and university education equally available to all Americans without regard to race, creed, sex, national origin, or economic status.

The proposed role, however, is not entirely a new one. For more than a century and a half the Federal Government has encouraged and supported specific fields of higher education and research. In times of national emergency it has expanded its support to give heightened recognition of the indispensable services which can be rendered to the Nation by the colleges and universities. But aid for a few specific needs and temporary action in times of crisis are not enough. *The time has come when the Federal Government must concern itself with the total and long-time needs for higher education. These needs are ever present and ever increasing. Higher education is no less important to the Nation in calmer times than in periods of national crisis.*

Although major emphasis in this volume has been given to the role of the Federal Government, this emphasis does not in any sense lessen the responsibility of local and State governments and of private interests in financing an adequate program of higher education. Indeed it is the firm conviction of this Commission that every effort must be exerted by the States and their subdivisions. The Commission is equally firm in its conviction, however, based on its study, that these needs are so great and so important that the maximum effort which may be reasonably expected from local and State governments will not be sufficient to provide all of the funds required to realize the complete program of higher education which the times demand. The role, therefore, proposed for the Federal Government is that of a partner — a partner jointly responsible with the States and localities for attaining the goals for higher education in a democracy.

The development of a carefully planned, well conceived, and cooperatively evolved program of higher education will entail a continuing study of national needs and resources and the relative role of both governmental and nongovernmental sources of income.

STATEMENT OF DISSENT

This statement of dissent is concerned primarily with the unqualified recommendation of the Commission that Federal funds for current expenditures and capital outlay be appropriated for use in publicly controlled institutions of higher education only. A careful review of the Commission's report as a whole has convinced us that this particular recommendation is inconsistent with other policies and proposals advocated by the Commission. Furthermore, the reasons proposed by the majority of the Commission in support of this recommendation are really nothing more than declarations that public colleges and universities must have a priority for Federal funds and that private institutions would be subjected to governmental control if they should accept Federal funds. These declarations do not furnish any valid support for the statement of a principle that, under no circumstances and regardless of State policies and practices, may Federal funds for current expenditures and capital outlay be provided to privately controlled institutions of higher education as such. Nowhere in the report are any sound reasons given on the basis of which privately controlled colleges and universities, which have had long and distinguished records of service to our Nation in peace and war, should be disqualified from the benefits of a Federal-aid program.

Before presenting in detail the reasons for our position, we wish to stress the point that our dissent is not a mere personal plea for the special interests of private education. A recent poll conducted by the American Council on Education revealed that 241 members, about half of those replying to the Council's questionnaire, voted in favor of the proposition that Federal funds be made available "to nonprofit private as well as to public education," including, therefore, privately and publicly controlled institutions of higher learning. And these votes, we have every reason to believe, were cast in the best interests of the general welfare. In light of this fact, we, as members of the Commission, are convinced that it is our duty to state to the President of the United States and to the American public that this drastic recommendation to bar private colleges and universities from receiving Federal funds does not reflect the thinking of the most representative cross section of American college and university leaders and will certainly have dangerous implications for the future welfare of both public and private higher education.

This recommendation, as we understand it, is based on a theory of educational finance which asserts that "public control" rather than "service to the public" shall be the sole criterion of a school's eligibility to receive public funds. Underlying this theory is the assumption that American democracy will be best served by a mighty system of public higher education to be financed by local, State, and Federal taxes, and to be controlled, managed, and supervised by governmental agencies. Accordingly, the Commission's report predicts — and without regrets — the gradual elimination of those private colleges and universities which are unable to keep pace with their publicly endowed competitors. The report also envisions the development of a Nationwide system of higher education in which private colleges and universities will play an increasingly minor role.

We believe it is timely in this connection to call attention to the dangers of a higher educational system largely or completely dominated by the State. Exclusive control of education, more than any other factor, made the dictatorships of Germany, Italy, and Japan acceptable to an ever-increasing number of their populations. The question immediately comes to mind whether American education can continue to withstand the modern social trend toward governmental domination of the educational process. We confess definite misgivings on this point, now that the Commission has so decisively recommended a monopoly of tax funds for publicly controlled colleges and universities. We fear that legislation implementing the Commission's recommendation would go a long way toward establishing an administrative structure for higher education whereby Government in the United States might easily use the Nation's public colleges and universities to promote its political purposes.

With respect to the report itself, we are unable to determine why the Commission recommended in such an unqualified fashion that no Federal funds for current expenditures and capital outlay be given to private institutions of higher learning. Throughout the report there are frequent references to the quasi-public functions performed by private colleges and universities, and repeatedly these institutions are praised for their achievements in serving the public welfare. We note also that the Commission had no hesitancy in recommending that private institutions should lower their fees, adopt certain personnel practices, accept contracts from the Government for specialized research, admit students who receive national scholarships and fellowships, and follow a policy of nondiscrimination in admitting members of minority groups. In the Commission's own words:

". . . It is becoming generally acknowledged that, despite a large measure of private control and private support, these institutions are vitally affected with the public interest. Not only is this reflected in the privilege of tax exemption which they are accorded, but also in the process of State accreditation in certain States, and in the recognition that they constitute part of a program of higher education dedicated to the Nation's welfare. They are thus genuinely vested with a public interest and as such are morally obligated to abandon all restrictive policies. . . ."

The Commission accordingly has decided that, although private institutions must render the same public service as do public schools, they shall receive none of the funds appropriated by Government as compensation for the public service rendered. This decision would appear to us as arbitrary, to say the least.

In making this recommendation, the Commission apparently lost sight of its primary purpose which was to propose ways and means of equalizing educational opportunity for higher education on a much broader basis than ever before in history and to provide for the expansion and development of educational facilities at the higher levels to meet the needs of a vastly increased number of students. In the light of this purpose, nothing could be more untimely, nothing more futilely doctrinaire than for this Commission to adopt a recommendation which would, in effect, destroy the happy balance and cordial relations which now exist in higher education, and which would cause many of our great private institutions to curtail expansion of facilities at a time when such expansion is absolutely necessary in terms of the general welfare.

We now turn our attention to the specific reasons allegedly supporting the recommendation to which we object. In our opinion, these reasons are either gratuitous or specious. The report declares that Government has "a prime responsibility" to provide opportunities for higher education and has a "fundamental obligation . . . to establish a sound system of public education and to support it to the fullest extent possible." The report also states that the discharge of this responsibility "does not deny in any way" the right of individuals to have and to support their own schools. We fail to see how it follows from these "reasons" that private institutions which are, as a matter of fact, cooperating with the Government by providing a "high quality" education for thousands of young men and women should be disqualified from receiving Federal aid.

We are not impressed by the Commission's admonition that the acceptance of Federal funds would expose private education to Federal control. The very same admonition might be directed to publicly controlled colleges and universities. As the report clearly indicates, it is the policy of the Commission that Federal aid to education must not impose upon the institutions assisted any form of Federal control over their academic or personnel practices. Furthermore, it is the considered judgment of the Commission that publicly controlled colleges and universities may accept Federal aid without submitting to any Federal dictation on their academic policies. There appears to be no reason why Federal aid to privately controlled institutions would entail a greater risk of Federal control than would similar aid to publicly controlled institutions. In practice, the amount of Federal aid to any institution would not be large enough to expose the institution to Federal control as ordinarily understood.

We submit that the criterion of a school's eligibility to receive Federal funds should be its "service to the public" and not "public control." Our position is based upon our conviction that American democracy will be best served if higher education in the future, as in the past, will continue to be regarded as a responsibility to be shared by public and private colleges and universities. This American tradition of democratic school administration suggests that the Government should be disposed to aid any qualified college or university, regardless of whether it is administered by a quasi-public body, like a board of trustees appointed by the State officials or elected by the people, or whether it is managed by a private nonprofit corporation. In no case should Government be conceded the right to measure its financial aid to an institution by the degree of control which it exercises over its administration. In the matter of control, the Government must be neutral. Its standard is "service to the public" and this standard squares with the American tradition of democracy in education.

That private colleges and universities do perform a public service is a fact beyond dispute. We see no reason why they should not continue and be helped to continue this service.

Msgr. FREDERICK G. HOCHWALT.
MARTIN R. P. McGUIRE.

James Bryant Conant:

EDUCATION FOR A CLASSLESS SOCIETY:
The Jeffersonian Tradition

THE United States was once proclaimed as the land of the free. Now we are more often reminded that it has been the profitable home of an acquisitive society. Greed and "lust for money," we are told, determined the course of development of even the first years of the republic.

Yet, as early as 1800 a potent but silent ferment was at work which had nothing to do with the almighty dollar. In describing conditions at the beginning of Jefferson's administration, Henry Adams writes as follows: "European travelers who passed through America noticed that everywhere, in the White House at Washington and in log cabins beyond the Alleghenies, except for a few Federalists, every American, from Jefferson and Gallatin down to the poorest squatter, seemed to nourish an idea that he was doing what he could to overthrow the tyranny which the past had fastened on the human mind." This idea so widely disseminated among the citizens of the raw republic of sixteen states seems to me one of the most essential and continuing elements in the development of American education. I have ventured to associate with this passion for freedom of the mind two other closely allied elements — namely, a belief in careers open to all through higher education, and a faith in universal schooling. I have labeled the whole with Jefferson's name.

I trust that neither his shade nor American historians will be unduly offended by my terminology.

In his brief autobiographical sketch Jefferson wrote that he deemed it essential to a well-ordered republic to annul hereditary privilege. He proposed "instead of an aristocracy of wealth, of more harm and danger, than benefit, to society, to make an opening for the aristocracy of virtue and talent, which nature has wisely provided for the direction of the interests of society, and scattered with equal hand through all its conditions. . . ." Elsewhere, in describing his new educational scheme for Virginia, he speaks of that part of his plan which called for "the selection of the youths of genius from among the classes of the poor." He declared, "We hope to avail the State of those talents which nature has sown as liberally among the poor as the rich, but which perish without use, if not sought for and cultivated." These quotations sum up for me the second component in the Jeffersonian tradition in education — a sincere belief in the paramount importance of careers freely open to all the talented.

Most important for its effect on the development of American educational practice was the third element of the tradition — Jefferson's devotion to the principle of universal schooling. This doctrine naturally has had more general popular

Reprinted by permission from *Atlantic Monthly*, CLXV, No. 5 (May, 1940), 593–602. James Bryant Conant is President, Harvard University.

appeal throughout the years than either concern for freedom of the mind or desire for opportunity through higher education. For here was a proposition which directly affected every family in the land. To quote from the proposal for Virginia, "The ultimate result of the whole scheme of education would be the teaching of *all* the children of the State reading, writing and common arithmetic. . . ." These words of Jefferson may now seem to us to describe a degree of general education so small as to be negligible. But when they were written they expressed a revolutionary doctrine — a belief that every potential citizen in a democratic republic should receive at least a minimum of formal instruction. The campaign against illiteracy had begun in earnest.

As a recent biographer has said, Jefferson believed that any boy or girl was capable of benefiting from the rudiments of education and would be made a better citizen by acquiring them. He believed in keeping open the door of further opportunity to the extent that a poor boy of ability should not be debarred from continuing his education. "To have gone farther and made a higher education compulsory on all," suggests this biographer, "would have seemed as absurd to him as to have decreed that every crop on his farm, whether tobacco, potatoes, rye, corn, or what not, must be treated and cultivated in precisely the same way as every other. . . . In terms of the citizen, he believed in the maximum of equality of opportunity. In terms of the state, he believed in the minimum of compulsion and interference compatible with the training of all its citizens as citizens to the maximum of the capacity of each."

To understand the bearing of Jefferson's ideas on the development of American schools and colleges we must realize, of course, that they represented only one aspect of a wider social philosophy. As this philosophy was understood by large numbers of the citizens of the young republic, it included the following points: a belligerent belief in individual freedom; complete confidence in the powers of man's intelligence to overcome all obstacles; the assumption of a society without hereditary classes, without an aristocracy; a differentiation of labors with a corresponding differentiation in the types of education (but no ruling caste, no hereditary educational privileges, everyone to be "as good as everyone else"); widespread education for all citizens so that political decisions might be "rational." Dominating all was the doctrine of the maximum independence of the individual, the minimum of social control by organized society. . . .

I venture to look forward to a renaissance of the vitality of the first element in the Jeffersonian tradition in education — freedom of the mind. I am equally optimistic about the second — equality of opportunity. I plead guilty at once to wishful thinking. Furthermore, I admit cheerfully that I propose to indulge in dangerous prophecy. But can anyone discuss the future with a neutral mind?

Until fairly recently it was taken for granted that the American republic could be described as classless. For a century and a half Americans have been saying with pride, "This is a free country. There are no classes in the United States." Note these words carefully, for the denial of classes in America is the denial of hereditary classes, not the denial of temporary groupings based on economic differences. "Caste" and "class" are equated by the average American, and I shall follow this usage. "This is a free country. There are no classes in the United States." The number of times these two sentences have been sincerely spoken could be recorded only by a figure of astronomical magnitude. Were they ever an approximately accurate description of typical American society? My answer would be yes. Have they today sufficient vitality and validity to be the basis for a continuation of Jefferson's educational program? A crystal gazer alone could tell. But I think the chance is good enough to demand our careful consideration of the possibility. For my own part, I risk with enthusiasm an affirmative answer and stand on the hope of our reconstituting a free and classless nation.

Phrases descriptive of a free, casteless, or classless society have not only represented an American belief of great potency in the past, but have described actual conditions in many sections of this republic. As compared with the situation in even such free countries as England and France, this country was unique in being without hereditary classes. The importance of this fact, I believe, has not been fully emphasized. But, I hasten to add, the social changes which have altered the situation during the last fifty years have all too often been ignored.

American society in some localities has always been organized on definite class lines; money and power have been passed on from father to son. The different strata have been relatively rigid and impenetrable. But until recently such situations were the exception rather than the rule. Now we see in progress the rapid extension of such stratification over the whole land. We see throughout the country the development of a hereditary aristocracy of wealth. The coming of modern industrialism and the passing of the frontier with cheap lands mark the change. Ruthless and greedy exploitation of both natural and human resources by a small privileged class founded on recently acquired ownership of property has hardened the social strata and threatens to provide explosive material beneath.

Let us not shut our eyes to the realities. The vanishing of free lands, the spread of large-scale manufacturing units, the growth of cities and their slums, the multiplication of tenant farmers and despairing migratory laborers, are signs of the passage from one type of social order to another. The existence of vast unemployment only emphasizes the evil significance of an unwelcome change. Have we reached a point where the ideal of a peculiar American society, classless and free, must be regarded as of only historical significance?

Our friends on the Left will, I imagine, say yes. A class struggle is inevitable, they declare. Forget the dreams of a pioneer civilization, the early American town or farm, and face the modern capitalistic world, they urge. From their viewpoint no discussion of present problems which refuses to fit every fact into the framework of a class struggle can be realistic. The extremists will add, at least to themselves, that the outcome of the struggle is also inevitable — a classless society, not of the early American type, but on the Russian model.

On the extreme Right we may find an equally clear renunciation of the ideal — equally clear, but not, as a rule, equally outspoken, for the underlying assumptions here are often entirely unconscious. Throughout the history of this republic there has been among a small group undue admiration for the educational system of England, a system built largely on class lines. Among such people Jefferson's idea of careers open to all the talented has evoked little enthusiasm. There has been little concern with recruiting the professions from every economic level.

The ideal has been education of a ruling caste rather than a selective system of training leaders.

Yet the unique character of the American way of life has been repeatedly emphasized since Jefferson's time. Lincoln in his first message to Congress declared that "the leading object of the Government for whose existence we contend" is "to elevate the condition of men; to lift artificial weights from all shoulders; to clear the paths of laudable pursuit for all; to afford all an unfettered start and a fair chance in the race of life." The historian, F. J. Turner, writing at the beginning of the present century, summed up the case as follows: "Western democracy through the whole of its earlier period tended to the production of a society of which the most distinctive fact was freedom of the individual to rise under conditions of social mobility. . . ."

Let me pause a moment to examine the phrase "social mobility," for this is the heart of my argument. A high degree of social mobility is the essence of the American ideal of a classless society. If large numbers of young people can develop their own capacities irrespective of the economic status of their parents, then social mobility is high. If, on the other hand, the future of a young man or woman is determined almost entirely by inherited privilege or the lack of it, social mobility is nonexistent. You are all familiar with the old American adage, "Three generations from shirt sleeves to shirt sleeves." This implies a high degree of social mobility, both up and down. It implies that sons and daughters must and can seek their own level, obtain their own economic rewards, engage in any occupation irrespective of what their parents might have done.

Contrast this adage with a statement of the aristocratic tradition — namely, that it takes three generations to educate a gentleman. Fifty years ago the contrast between these two statements would have been proclaimed by many intelligent Americans as the epitome of the difference between the New World and the Old. The possibility that each generation may start life afresh and that hard work and ability would find their just rewards was once an exciting new doctrine. Is it outworn? In short, has the second component of the Jeffersonian tradition in education still vitality? Can a relatively high degree of social mobility be realized in this modern world?

The distinction between a stratified class system and one with a high degree of social mobility is apparent only when at least two generations are passed in review. A class, as I am using the word, is perpetuated by virtue of inherited position. For one generation, at least, and perhaps two, considerable differences in economic status as well as extreme differentiation of employment may exist without the formation of classes. Uniform distribution of the world's goods is not necessary for a classless society. If anyone doubts this statement, let him examine the social situation of many small communities in different parts of this country during the early stages of their development. Continuous perpetuation from generation to generation of even small differences, however, soon produces class consciousness. Extremes of wealth or poverty accelerate the process.

It is not within my province to consider what political measures should be taken if we reject the idea of an inevitable stratification of society. It is not for me to say what legislation is in order if we desire to implement the ideal of a free classless society. My unwillingness to discuss this important aspect of the problem is not to be taken as a measure of my dissatisfaction with the rapidly growing social and economic differentiation of the United States. On the contrary, if the American ideal is not to be an illusion, the citizens of this republic must not shrink from drastic action. The requirement, however, is not a radical equalization of wealth at any given moment; it is rather a continuous process by which power and privilege may be automatically redistributed at the end of each generation. The aim is a more equitable distribution of opportunity for all the children of the land. The reality of our national life must be made a sufficiently close approximation to our ideal to vitalize a belief in the possibility of the envisaged goal.

I am wary of definitions — even in expounding the exact sciences to an elementary class. It is often more profitable to explain the nature of a concept by illustration than to attempt a definition. Both the words "free" and "classless," as I am employing them, have a relative, not an absolute, meaning. They are useful, I believe, even in a rough quantitative sense, in contrasting different types of social organizations which have existed in the last few centuries in the Western World. It is easy to imagine a small segment of any country where one would be hard put to it to say whether the society in question was free and classless, or the contrary. To pass a judgment on larger social units is even more difficult, but I should not hesitate to say that Russia today is classless, but not free; England free, but not classless; Germany neither free nor classless.

To contrast the social history of the United States and that of even so closely related a country as Great Britain is illuminating. If we examine, for example, the recent history by G. D. H. Cole entitled *The British Common People*,

1746–1938, we shall see portrayed the evolution of one type of political democracy within a highly stratified caste system. Compare this picture with the history of the growth of this republic by expansion through the frontier in the last one hundred years — a history in which social castes can be ignored; a history where, by and large, opportunity awaited the able and daring youths of each new generation.

This fundamental difference between the United States and England has been blurred by similarities in our political and legal systems and by our common literary culture. Failure to give due weight to the differences between a casteless society and a stratified society has had unfortunate consequences for our thinking. I have already suggested that many of our friends on the Right have had their educational views distorted by too ardent contemplation of the English public schools (so-called) and English universities. Similarly, I believe that in the last few decades our friends on the Left, who look towards a collectivist society, have suffered from overexposure to British views — views emanating in this case not from the ruling class but from the left-wing intellectuals of the Labor Party. It seems to me that in this century, as in a much earlier period of our history, an imported social philosophy has strongly influenced radical thought. I am not referring to orthodox Marxism, but rather to the general slant of mind inevitable among English and Continental reformers whose basis of reference is a society organized on hard-and-fast class lines. The original American radical tradition has been given a twist by the impact of these alien ideas. As far as the role of government is concerned, the political reformer has swung completely round the circle. On this issue, Jefferson with his almost anarchistic views would find difficulty, indeed, in comprehending his modern political heirs.

Native American radicalism has all but disappeared. Our young people now seem forced to choose between potential Bourbons and latent Bolsheviks. But without a restoration of the earlier type of radical the Jeffersonian tradition in education will soon die. Obviously it cannot long survive a victory of the socialistic Left — there is no place for such ideas in a classless society on the Russian model. And it will likewise disappear automatically unless a high degree of social mobility is once again restored. To keep society fluid, the honest and sincere radical is an all-important element. Those in positions of power and privilege (including college presidents) need to be under constant vigilant scrutiny and from time to time must be the objects of attack. Tyrannies of ownership and management spring up all too readily. In order to ensure that the malignant growths of the body politic will be destroyed by radiations from the Left, much abuse of healthy and sound tissue must be endured. Reformers and even fanatical radicals we must have. But if the unique type of American society is to continue, those who would better conditions must look in the direction of the progressive or liberal movements of an earlier period. The Left must consider returning to the aim of checking tyranny and restoring social mobility. Reformers must examine every action lest they end by placing in power the greatest tyrant of all — organized society.

There are probably some who feel that I am indulging in nostalgic fancy when I hope for the evolution of a less stratified and more fluid society. You may say that the modern world of large cities, vast industries, and scientific methods of communication has made the America of a hundred years ago as irrelevant as the Middle Ages. You may argue that a way of life which was possible in the 1840's is impossible in the 1940's; that in the near future we shall all of us have to move in a quite contrary direction. You may contend that soon we shall have to take sides in a bitter class struggle and choose between an American brand of Fascism and an American brand of Socialism.

I know that many believe this to be inevitable. I venture to disagree. And here is the reason for my rash dissent. In my opinion, our newly erected system of public education has potentialities of which we little dream. In this century we have erected a new type of social instrument. Our secondary-school system is a vast engine which we are only beginning to understand. We are learning only slowly how to operate it for the public good. But I have hope that it will aid us in recapturing social flexibility, in regaining that great gift to each succeeding generation — opportunity, a gift that once was the promise of the frontier.

Let me explain. Today some six million boys and girls attend our secondary schools, ten times the number enrolled a half century ago. Today nearly three quarters of those of high-school age are enrolled as pupils; fifty years ago schooling at this level was a privilege of less than ten per cent of those who might attend. Opportunity can be evaluated only in terms of personal capacity. What is opportunity for one young man is a blind alley for another. In rapidly expanding pioneer communities, openings for capabilities of all sorts automatically appeared. Only doctors, lawyers, and ministers needed an extensive education.

Opportunities were ready at hand for all other types of talent. In our highly industrialized, relatively static society, the situation is otherwise. The personal problem of each boy or girl is much more difficult. Abilities must be assessed, talents must be developed, ambitions guided. This is the task for our public schools. All the future citizens pass through these institutions. They must be educated as members of a political democracy, but, more important still, they must be equipped to step on to the first rung of whatever ladder of opportunity seems most appropriate. And an appropriate ladder must be found for each one of a diverse group of students. This may seem an overwhelming burden to put upon our educational system. But is it not possible that our public schools, particularly our high schools, can be reconstructed for this specific purpose?

Jefferson thought of universal schooling of younger children chiefly in terms of educating potential voters. His selective process for higher studies was conceived in terms of intellectual pursuits — of preparation for the learned professions such as law and medicine. To continue the tradition he started, we must expand both of his ideas today. The roads which lead to those careers which depend on aptitude for "book learning" still run through the universities. We must fight to keep them open. State-supported universities have blazed the way. But the task is far from done. In many localities the opportunities for the children of the really poor are lamentable indeed. Outside of metropolitan areas and college towns, the privileges of a professional training are hard to win. An expanded scholarship policy in our privately endowed universities is imperative. Wisely administered student aid will go far to right the balance. Perhaps this device

merits more attention even by institutions supported by the state.

The changes required to provide adequately for the intellectually gifted are relatively slight. The real problems of reconstruction of our schools and colleges do not lie in this area. The real difficulties are with the careers of a different sort. Our schools must be concerned with educating for a useful life a great variety of boys and girls. They must be concerned not only with the able scholar, but with the artist and the craftsman. They must nourish those whose eye or ear or manual dexterity is their greatest asset. They must educate others whose gifts lie in an ability to understand and lead their fellow men. The school curricula must include programs for developing the capacities of many who possess intuitive judgment on practical affairs but have little or no aptitude for learning through the printed page.

It has been a natural consequence of our history that many false values now permeate the entire educational system. "Book learning" is placed too high in the scale of social ratings by some; too low by others who profess to scoff at "brains." That type of ability which can handle easily the old-fashioned subjects of the curriculum is often glorified by being equated with "intelligence" by educational snobs. On the other hand, the same ability often suffers from lack of stimulation when there is failure to maintain high standards. As a result, we have a great deal of make-believe in our schools and colleges — too many feeble attempts at tasks which are proper only for a restricted type of individual; too many failures to explore talents which fall outside orthodox academic bounds. Jefferson in the simpler society of his day naturally thought of only a few avenues of opportunity open through education. Today we must recognize the existence of many and strive for the social equality of all.

Parents who expect miracles worked upon their children must be reminded of the limitations imposed by nature. In athletics, at least, the coaches are expected to develop only promising material. No one complains if his undersized son with awkward legs does not become a football hero. Some fathers, however, seem to demand the intellectual equivalent of such a miracle. We expect our college health departments to direct each student into that form of sport which is suited to his physique and power. We need a parallel form of educational guidance in both schools and colleges to assist the development of the skills of brain and hands.

But again I venture to be optimistic. I see signs everywhere of enormous strides forward in such matters. Our educational pattern is becoming daily more diversified; a recognition of the need for a radically different type of education is growing. We look forward to the opening of many channels which lead to a variety of attractive goals; we can envisage the building up of more than one "elite."

Of course, in any realistic discussion of these problems we cannot neglect the social and economic factors. As long as the shadow of unemployment is upon the land, some method of providing food and clothing for the children of many families must be found. For even free schools offer little real opportunity to famished youngsters; public education is only theoretically available to those in rags. Providing food and clothing for those to whom assistance is essential is clearly necessary for a satisfactory functioning of the entire educational system. Many a talented youth is lost by dropping out of the competition, for financial reasons, during the high-school years. In short,

we must explore every method of developing the individual capacity of each future citizen for useful labor based on individual initiative.

Political and economic changes must go hand in hand with educational innovations — the revision of methods of perpetuating control of many large industries, the overthrow of nepotism and patronage wherever possible, the stimulation of small enterprises, the spreading of private ownership. All this and more is needed if a free classless society is to become once again an ideal which affects our lives.

Freedom of the mind, social mobility through education, universal schooling — these, let me repeat, are the three fundamentals of the Jeffersonian tradition. They have represented the aspirations and desires of a free people embarked on a new experiment, the perpetuation of a casteless nation. Popular enthusiasm for enlightenment, for over-turning dogmas, for intellectual exploration, has temporarily waned. I have given my reasons for hoping that the black reaction of these years is only a passing phase. The ideal of a free republic without classes has likewise suffered an eclipse. To many of the present college generation the phrase "equality of opportunity" seems a mockery, a trite collection of idle words. In this I see the major challenge to our educational system, a challenge which can be met only by a radical reconstruction. If the nation wants to bend its efforts to have as free and classless a society *as possible,* then for those of us concerned with schools and colleges our course is clearly plotted.

So it seems to me. If we as educators accept the American ideal, then this acceptance must be the major premise for all our thinking. Without neglecting the older roads designed for those of academic brilliance, we must construct many new approaches to adult life, and we must do so very soon. Extreme differentiation of school programs seems essential — differentiation of instruction, but not necessarily a division into separate schools. From this it follows that rapid improvement in our testing methods must be forthcoming; a much more conscientious and discriminating form of educational guidance must be developed soon if we are not to fail. In short, a horde of heterogeneous students has descended on our secondary schools; on our ability to handle all types intelligently depends in large measure the future of this country.

Is it too late — too late for our schools to revitalize the idea of a classless nation? Can we complete the necessary major readjustments in our educational system in time to prevent the extinction of the Jeffersonian tradition? I believe we can, if we make haste. I predict at least an-

other century of vigor for the American ideal. I envisage a further trial on this continent for many generations of our unique type of social order. I look forward to a future American society in which social mobility is sufficient to keep the nation in essence casteless — a society in which the ideals of both personal liberty and social justice can be maintained — a society which through a system of public education resists the distorting pressures of urbanized, industrial life. I have faith in the continuation of a republic composed of citizens each prepared to shoulder the responsibility for his own destiny. And if at each step in the educational journey opportunity truly beckons, will not each student rejoice in the struggle to develop his own capacities? Will he not be proud of the continuing American tradition and find in contemplation of our national history ample courage to face those risks and hazards that come to all who would be free?

Robert S. Lynd: WHO CALLS THE TUNE?

"Establishing the Goals," Volume I of the "Report of the President's Commission on Higher Education"

EDUCATORS, of all people, should be most apt at seeing things whole, with parts observed in relation to the biasing over-all thrust of the whole system. It is we who are most vocal about the "total situation," the "whole personality," the continuities involved in "activity

leading to further activity," and similar emphases on wholeness, interaction of parts, and the dynamics of growth, movement, and change.

Of course, anything must be temporarily abstracted and in some sense distorted in order to be studied at all. One

Reprinted by permission from *Journal of Higher Education*, XIX (April, 1948), 163–174. Robert S. Lynd is Professor of Sociology, Columbia University.

fixates upon any given thing under discussion, precisely as one focuses a camera or a microscope; and this process in some sense temporarily plays down the rest of the universe. Any field of science or action gets ahead with its proper business largely by concentrating on things interior to itself. This is why we must have division of labor among our specialties. But recurrently, and especially at the times when one resets goals for future work, it is relevant to ask: How does the rest of what is going on in the social universe outside my specialty impinge upon what I am trying to do and upon the way I state my problems?

The significance of the interrupting pressure of the rest of the social world upon the component parts of a social system and its culture varies with time and location. For long stretches of time in earlier eras, peasants off the main trade routes lived and died in what to our hurtling institutional world seems an incredible localization and homely fixity of circumstances; one's life was pressed very close to the exigent immediacies of nature, with few interruptions from without. Even those of us in our fifties who grew up in Middle Western small towns can remember the quiet, leisurely tempo of a largely self-contained world of local affairs. Progress was manifestly happening, but it was a benign progress, with the scenery cut to the size of ordinary people. Democracy, too, was surely happening, unchallenged and here to stay. And business was the great wheel that bore everything forward. One did not hear the word *ideology* in those days, and while there was occasional "labor trouble," were we not all Americans and would not each of us get "his turn" if he worked hard? Today we are living in an ideological devil's cauldron, with ourselves and all our values tossed about and

obscured. This, we are beginning reluctantly to realize, is one of the great historic eras of institutional change, one of the decisive moments of human history. It is a time when the institutional chunks of our culture grind against each other in a movement so vast as to dwarf the individual. Never before in our national life have the will and the voice of the single man of integrity and good will seemed so impotent; only group action any longer counts for social change, and the middle-class man can find no group with whom to move except those carrying old banners in dubious directions.

In times like these, what is the case with those who assay to talk about education? Can one in these days talk about things of the mind and spirit as worthy in themselves? Surely one must — now more than ever! And yet one has an eerie sense of whistling in the wind. Education, we say, must be related to life. But to which part of this roaring hurricane of reality that besets us? Deep in our cultural tradition is the conception of "natural order" and a "higher sanction" underlying the daily circumstances of social living. On such an assumption "education" makes sense; for one learns about things that are surely there, in place, moving with one to appointed, though perhaps not yet entirely apparent, goals. One can teach and one can learn, even as one can "belong," in a world so conceived. Education can view itself as in some real sense belonging to itself, an autonomous permanent force authorized to state values for society and to work steadily to make those values real in daily life. In a world so conceived there is "sin" and there are "good" people and "bad" people; but the universe is neither sinful nor aimless, and democracy is not at stake; and the grand adventure of education, working with the tide of the universe and of democracy, is to make more and more people more rational (that is, "better") until the underlying drive toward orderliness comes to pervade all men's affairs. Here is a setting for confidence for the educator.

And it is this kind of confident statement of its own goals that the opening volume on *Establishing the Goals* of the "Report of the President's Commission on Higher Education" makes — and makes superbly. I happen not to be an enthusiast for the new gospel of "general education," and I became somewhat restless when the Report moved on to that specific recommendation, for reasons I shall state later in this paper.* But the first two chapters on the broad aims of education state better than I have ever seen them stated before what every imaginative educator dreams of at his healthiest, most rested, professional best. . . .

I read these pages with the sustained inner excitement that accompanies the clear public affirmation in an important document of the values one affirms most deeply in a time of controversy. But even as I read, I had a troubled sense of indulgence in unreality, of something vital left out. The experience reverberated other similar experiences — college chapel services that had caught me up momentarily into singleness of focus, and a memorable service on the day of the Assumption in Chartres Cathedral from which it had been a shock to come out into the August sunlight of the "other world" outside.

It is this bifocal quality about reading such contemporary statements of the "goals of education" that worries me; the insistent presence of "another world outside"; and the persistent, interrupting sense that our fine educational talk, hon-

* [Professor Lynd's criticisms of "general education" have been omitted for lack of space. Ed.]

est as it is, is turned into "double-talk" by things beyond the control of us educators.

I have already said that, if one can assume a natural goodness and orderliness in the universe directly related to men's constructive efforts, it makes sense for education to state its own orderly, autonomous aims and to seek to realize them. But this assumption does not hold. There is no basic orderliness in social living; our institutions have no "higher" validation, but are what they have come to be — man-made and subject to all the vicissitudes of time and circumstance; and education, far from occupying an ordained place in the human procession, is only what it can contrive to be in the jostling throng of interests that seek to have things their own way in society.

It is good to be confident. Chapter I of the "Report of the President's Commission" is headed "Education for a Better Nation and a Better World," and the closing subhead of the chapter is "It Can Be Done." The only hindrances seen by the Commission are internal to education itself:

[These goals] pose a truly staggering job for the colleges and universities. But it can be done. The necessary intelligence and ability exist. What we need is awareness of the urgency of the task, and the will and courage to tackle it, and a wholehearted commitment to its successful performance (page 23).

But the sober fact dogs the work of all of us who value democracy and the sensitive aspects of human living that "intelligence," "awareness of the urgency of the task," and "will and courage" on the part of us educators still may not be enough to force the door through which we must pass to achieve our goals. It is, therefore, the stark realities of the institutional setting in which education, the family, democracy, and our other institutional foci of values are caught today that must be studied first by those who seek to state and to realize values.

The weakness of the "Report of the President's Commission on Higher Education" is that it states a program for education apart from a realistic appraisal of the nature and drive of power in the contemporary United States.

The simple fact — to which we educators pay formal lip service in our troubled private discussions among ourselves — is that education may not look upon itself as an independent force in society. We non-Catholics worry about the case of education forced to operate within the political goals of the organization ramifying from the Vatican. But we do not, in the main and in public, recognize the possibility that there are other constraints upon education no less coercive and determined to have their way within our own cultural system. Our general confidence about education in America stems from the fact that we assume the dominant characteristic of our society to be that it is a political democracy; that is, that the front door is open to Americans to do anything with our common life that the majority of us elect. But we must face the further question as to whether political democracy is, in fact, master in its own house. As Harold J. Laski points out in his *Democracy in Crisis:*

The Industrial Revolution brought the middle classes to power, and they evolved a form of state — capitalist democracy — which seemed most suited to their security. . . . It offered a share in political authority to all citizens upon the unstated assumption that the equality involved in the democratic ideal did not seek extension to the economic sphere. The assumption could not be maintained. . . .

[For the citizens, having won formal political power,] realized that the clue to authority lay in the possession of economic control. When they sought to move by the ordinary constitutional means to its conquest as well, they found that the fight had to be begun all over again. Not only was this the case, but the essential weapons lay in their opponents' hands. The Courts, the Press, the educational system, the armed forces of the state, even, in large degree, the bureaucracy, were instruments operating towards their defeat. If they maintained law and order, they maintained that subtle atmosphere upon which the security of economic privilege depended.[1]

What this suggests is that liberal democracy lives in unresolved conflict with capitalism. Charles A. Beard pointed out this basic ambivalence between our political and economic institutions in his *An Economic Interpretation of the Constitution of the United States.*[2] Our middle-class revolution, like the English revolution of the seventeenth century, failed to go clear through from the political to the economic sector, but ended in a makeshift compromise. This compromise has never been resolved, but has persisted as a more or less disguised guerilla warfare between the two fundamentally opposed segments of the culture.

Under the surface of our national life this irrepressible conflict has grown in violence with the unchecked increase in economic monopoly. Chapter 22 of Arthur Schlesinger, Jr.'s *The Age of Jackson*[3] deals with one of the occasions on which the issue broke into the open. It describes the re-forming of the fighting front of the predecessors of the present Republican party after their defeat by

[1] Chapel Hill, North Carolina: University of North Carolina Press, 1933, pp. 52–53.

[2] New York: Macmillan Company, 1913.

[3] Boston: Little, Brown and Company, 1945.

Andrew Jackson. The blunt emphasis of the financial and industrial upper class upon the fact that the masses were dangerous to property had proved in Jackson's campaign a double-edged weapon; for the masses, come to power, could claim that property was dangerous to the masses. So the aristocratic Whig party did a smart ideological face-lifting job, commencing in the 1830's. Central in this was the emphasis that America is different from Europe, class differences do not apply here, and the interests of all elements in our American population are identical. And, ever since, this line has proved a useful propaganda weapon for big business. One follows this struggle between democracy and capitalism through the fruitless effort to curb the monopoly tendency; the three revealing lobby investigations which have resulted in no check on the growing power of business lobbies; the fiasco of NRA which revealed that, when business is given its head even in a national emergency, it proceeds to have a field day for its own profit; the Nye Committee munitions investigation; the La Follette Committee investigation of the anti-labor tactics of big business; the business sabotaging of conversion to a wartime footing; the colossal profits of both World Wars; the killing of OPA by the National Association of Manufacturers; and so on.[4]

Today, big business, better organized than ever before and commanding all the best manipulative brains-for-sale in America, has launched an all-out campaign to shatter organized labor and to control political democracy through gaining command over public opinion at the grass roots. Central in this campaign is the false assertion that democracy and the "private enterprise system" are but two aspects of the same thing, and that democracy itself will collapse if the private-enterprise system is impaired. According to *Management News*, the organ of the American Management Association,

... probably more millions are being spent on public relations on behalf of the free enterprise system than management and stockholders realize. Virtually every industry in the United States — even the smallest companies — is involved in some effort to sell "economic truths" to the public.[5]

On February 1 of this year, a detailed plan, worked out by the best public-relations talent in the country, was thrown into gear to capture local communities for big business. This program calls for the systematic organization, first, of all the leaders at the local community level, from business through religion and education to labor; and then, through them, the organization of all the organizations in each community behind the purposes of business. What all of this means is that business is out to destroy the *private* character of everything except property. We educators may smile at *Trends in Education-Industry Cooperation*, sent us monthly by the NAM. But we do not smile at the systematic encirclement of free opinion that has put liberal commentators off the air, that suppresses and distorts important news in our press and periodicals,[6] or at the growing aggressiveness of businessmen alumni and

---

[4] Parts of the story are told in such books as Engelbrecht and Hanighen's *Merchants of Death*, Lundberg's *America's 60 Families*, I. F. Stone's *Business as Usual*, Carl Dreher's *The Coming Showdown*, George Seldes' *One Thousand Americans*, the La Follette Committee reports, and the publications of the Temporary National Economic Committee, especially Monograph 26 on *Economic Power and Political Pressures*.

[5] "The President's Scratch-Pad," Sept. 30, 1947.

[6] *See* the weekly issues of *In Fact*.

members of school boards and the organized heresy-hunting that is reaching shamelessly into our schools.

Here is the hard core of contemporary power that we educators must try to appraise and to hold relentlessly before ourselves as we look ahead. The issue does not concern "good" men and "bad" men. As William Allen White wrote in 1943 of the disenchanting spectacle in Washington:

> For the most part these managerial magnates are decent, patriotic Americans. . . . If you touch them in nine relations of life out of ten, they are kindly, courteous, Christian gentlemen.
>
> But in the tenth relation, where it touches their own organization, they are stark mad, ruthless, unchecked by God or man, paranoiacs, in fact, as evil in their design as Hitler.[7]

And it so happens that this tenth relation is the one that dominates American life. As educators confront it, the issue is not, as I say, one of "good" and "bad" men, but of private business as an *organized system of power*. It is the dynamic purposes of this system that confront us as we attempt to state the goals of education.

Why have Americans, proud as we are of our democracy, allowed this conflict within our house to go unresolved and now to mount to its present pitch of intensity? From the beginning of our national life we have leaned back upon natural law, natural rights, and progress. Having set up the external forms of democracy, we turned to the vast private adventure of growing rich. A great continent rich in resources beckoned, and the new power of machinery born of the Industrial Revolution lay ready to hand. With no threatening neighbors on this hemisphere, it seemed that we could al-

most literally throw the reins on the back of the democratic nag and let political progress happen, while we all attended to growing rich. Cheap European labor came here at its own expense, and we fed their bodies into the industrial furnace as we broke the plains, rolled steel rails, and built our cities.[8] Actually, all down through our national life, until only two decades ago, we were borne forward by a favoring tail wind. We did not appraise this as a sheer stroke of good fortune, but as a continuing vindication of the rightness and essential finality of our "American way" and its institutions. Only since 1929 have many Americans begun to suspect that progress is not a permanent, built-in part of the American scene.

Meanwhile, the depression of 1929 and after has alerted business power to the fact that all is not well with the private-enterprise system. The depression really hurt it, hurt it as nothing had hurt it before. And when the government moved in on business in the New Deal, business became thoroughly aroused. Government sponsorship of labor organization was a body blow; but, as noted in the Report to Executives on "Management Looks at the Labor Problem," it was government under the New Deal that had hurt property more than had labor.[9] So, today, government is the prize, the game is "for keeps," and business is in Washington to stay, with the armed forces as its closest ally. I do not believe that business will allow another New Deal, with its free-wheeling populist sentiment, to happen. As to the new strength of organized labor, this should be borne in mind: Next to, and as an adjunct to, control of the government, organized business today is out to destroy organized labor power; and

---

[7] From the *Emporia Gazette*. Quoted in Seldes, *op. cit.*, p. 150.

[8] See Sprague's *The Battle for Chicago* for the mood of this vast era of predation.

[9] *Business Week*, September 26, 1942.

despite the growth of organized labor from less than four million in 1932 to fourteen to fifteen million today, I believe the estimate may be hazarded that the *relative* position of labor in the power struggle today is weaker than it was twenty years ago. The development of labor-management training centers in our universities is a deceptive device aimed at pulling the teeth of potential leaders. This is industry's answer to the dangerous dilemma pointed out by Gunnar Myrdal in his *An American Dilemma*.[10] According to Myrdal, vertical mobility of able men out of the working class is being slowed up in America, but meanwhile increasing popular education is making these men better equipped to exercise leadership. If, he says, they are blocked from moving up in the industrial structure, they will in time turn to leadership of their own class.[11]

What all this means for education is serious in the extreme. It looks as though the old liberal middle way is out from here on: either democracy will arouse itself and move in on our economy and democratize it, or business will swallow up democracy — in which event we shall have an American version of fascism. There is evidence that, while the broad middle-class element in America has failed to learn any clear thing from the last two decades and still repeats mechanically and uncritically the slogans "freedom," "equality," and "competition," big business has been learning rapidly; and central in this new learning is a

fundamental administrative contempt for democracy as too slow, too unreliable, and too wasteful for the purposes of big business.[12]

The basis for my uneasiness about the goals for higher education stated in the "Report of the President's Commission" will by now be quite apparent. These goals are stated in the expansive mood of nineteenth-century liberalism. They are stated as education's own contribution to progress. And only the atom bomb is allowed to creep into the Report as a possible interruption of that progress. As a matter of fact, we Americans, including the President's Commission, have allowed ourselves to be stampeded by the atom bomb. Of course it has horrifyingly dangerous potentialities, but so do other achievements of modern science. It is also one of the great potentials for doing the work of men more quickly and economically. The thing that makes atomic energy dangerous is not the fact of its discovery, but the fact that a capitalist society views it primarily as a weapon in the world-wide struggle for power. And it is the failure of the President's Commission to identify correctly the prime destructive agent in the present scene that worries me.

The Commission is careful, with one exception, not to use the word *class*. We are a class-stratified society, as every capitalist society is, but the Commission struggles to avoid saying so. It hints at the problem when it says, "all too often the benefits of education have been sought and used for personal and private profit, to the neglect of public and social service" (page 10); and "nor can any

---

[10] New York: Harper and Brothers, 1944, p. 715.

[11] Of interest in this connection is the recent Luckman proposal that a million dollars a year be spent by industry on the education of labor-management leaders in colleges and universities, under an arrangement whereby labor and management would each nominate five hundred likely leaders annually for such indoctrination training.

[12] The new business tactic of the administrative by-passing of democracy at the level of government action is suggested in Walton Hamilton's "The Smoldering Constitutional Crisis," *New Republic*, January 18, 1943.

group in our society, organized or un-organized, pursue purely private ends and seek to promote its own welfare without regard to the social consequences of its activities" (page 10); and it identifies the fact of class by name in the passage quoted earlier from page 36 of the Report.

Throughout the volume, the implication is that our American system is essentially sound and requires only to be extended and corrected in respect to details. We are told that

. . . citizens need to understand thoroughly the functioning of political parties, the role of lobbies and pressure groups, the processes of ward and precinct caucuses. They need to know not only the potential greatness of democracy, not only the splendor of its aspirations, but also its present imperfections in practice (page 12).

And if students are taught that, despite the copious revelations of three Congressional lobbying investigations, lobbying flourishes in Washington and in our state capitals as never before and dominates legislation, then what? And when students seeking to "understand thoroughly the functioning of political parties" are confronted with a university or college administration that hesitates to let Henry Wallace speak on the campus, then what?

The Commission states that "perhaps" (and the qualification is significant) education's "most important role is to serve as an instrument of social transition" (page 6). And what are liberal students and faculty members to make of the obvious anxiety with which their administrative officers view their activities?

Again, the Commission speaks of the obvious fact that "the gap between our scientific know-how and our personal and social wisdom has been growing steadily through the years" (page 21). I wish the Commission had gone on to ask why this

is happening. It is not just a matter of the gap between the discovery and control of the use of atomic energy. No social scientist who believes in the need to close this gap and effect social change works on any campus without some degree of real anxiety as to the relation of his research and teaching to his chances of promotion; and this anxiety is directly mediated to him through the administration of the institution in which he teaches. I wish the Commission had read the first twenty-five pages of the TNEC Monograph 26 on *Economic Power and Political Pressures*.[13] This states better than any other source I know, the fact of the monopoly over science, both pure and applied, enjoyed by private business, and the resulting key political power in American life this gives to business. What I am trying to say is that the cause of the "gap" between what we know and what we elect or are able to apply is not the inadequacy of scientists in our colleges and universities, but the power of private business. In this connection, the Commission might also have read with profit pages 39 to 66 of the National Resources Committee's *Technological Trends and National Policy*, dealing with such things as business' resistance to the use of new scientific knowledge.[14]

Discrimination within American society is viewed by the Commission as a matter requiring changed attitudes. Of course it does. But how are we to bring about this change? There is good reason for saying that as long as the Negro is a marginal economic man in our society, to be used in times of labor shortage and fired when the labor market gets "easy," he will be discriminated against; and that

[13] United States Government Printing Office, 1941.
[14] United States Government Printing Office, 1937.

the "Jewish problem" is a function of an economy of artificial scarcity in which the Jew is a convenient scapegoat. As an educator and scientist, I feel "sold short" by a commission of my colleagues that leaves a problem like this hanging on the easy, vague basis of "changing attitudes."

And finally, the failure of the Commission boldly to "go to town" on the cause of the class basis for current higher education leaves me limp. Do they actually believe that within a class-stratified society there is any possibility of meeting their pious goal? They say that "even in the State-supported institutions we have been moving away from the principle of free education to a much greater degree than is commonly supposed" (page 28). If this is the case, it reflects strong pressures within our kind of society. Then how does the Commission conceive of a reversal of this tendency? Here again we face the puny strength of exhortation in the face of economic power.

A basic weakness of the Commission lies in its assumption that problems are discrete things to be "reconciled" one at a time, whereas the essence of the problem education confronts is a related *system* of power directives. We are told that "effective democratic education will deal directly with current problems" (page 6). But it makes no sense to tackle the subsidiary aspects of our culture apart from the central source of our dilemma. . . .

If all of this seems somewhat sharp in its critical stance, let me simply say this in conclusion: I write as a professor in a graduate school, and my central drive is to attempt to make "education" mean the responsibility of trained men and women to address themselves to fundamentally needed social change, whether as teachers or researchers or both. As such a teacher, I work constantly under the

shadow of the pliancy of American university administrators to business pressures, though I am fortunate in the case of my immediate university connection. It is just because I am so keenly aware of the need for more and more legislative appropriations and endowments, and aware of what this does to anxious administrators, that the failure of the Commission to address itself squarely to the problems of power in our society leaves me with a feeling of having been let down by my professional colleagues on the Commission.

The prospect ahead, as the reader will have gathered, seems to me more than a little dark and threatening. I see no ready solution to the dilemma of American education, caught, as I believe it is, ever more firmly in the vise of big-business power. As an educator and one who believes that democracy is one of the great social inventions glimpsed by man and, as such, worth fighting to preserve and perfect, I nevertheless believe that our first task is to try unflinchingly to understand and to state the full measure of the danger in which democracy and education lie. It helps neither democracy nor education to play the ostrich or to rest back upon optimism in a time like this.

The administrative echelons in our colleges and universities are most immediately the captives of business. This exposed position of the men who must deal directly with businessmen alumni, legislative committees, and private donors must be faced in all understanding and sympathy by the rest of us.

Next in the hierarchy come we members of the teaching staffs. Shorn of the defenses of administrative expediency which the officers above us may invoke, and directly pledged to the inner integrities of teaching as a profession, we face, for the most part one by one, the full brunt of outside opposition. Our defenses as teachers are not by any means negligible, but I believe that they are growing weaker. If we elect so to do, we can pull in our necks and teach the safe, non-political aspects of our respective subject-matters. Without minimizing our desperate need for all the generous and courageous support and protection administrators above us can give us, we may not rely on such support; nor may we take our color from our administrators. To do the latter of these is to quit-claim our central responsibility as teachers. Regardless of what administrators may do, courage must dig itself in at the level of the teaching ranks. And those of us who are full professors and in major institutions must be prepared to carry a disproportionate share of the fight in behalf of our less secure younger colleagues in the lower academic ranks and in behalf of those in smaller and more exposed institutions. Meanwhile, those of us who as social scientists work in the full heat of current issues require all of the understanding and assistance we can get from our colleagues in less controversial fields like the humanities and the natural sciences. One of the ominous symptoms on many campuses today is the quiet withdrawal from colleagues who get the increasingly easy label, "radical."

Along with teachers come the students. It is my definite impression that this postwar student body, as I meet them in the graduate school, is the best I have ever known — with an extraordi-

nary level of social realism and readiness to face the facts. I have never before had so many students ready to ask, "All right, if this is the situation, where can I go out and get to work on the problem of democracy?" The answer to that one wrings the vitals of the candid professor! It is my belief that education must rely as never before upon the fresh thrust of energy and courage of our students as an indispensable ally. Our respect for our students and what they can contribute must rise in these critical times to levels perhaps never before reached.

And now, turning the Commission's affirmation into a question: Can it be done? None of us knows, but none of us can afford to quit the fight. Each time an administrator stands unwaveringly between a professor or students and outside attack, the democratic tradition survives in that action. A teacher stands before his class or confers with a student in his office and gives his whole self — his doubts, his lack of knowledge, as well as his affirmations — and, again, the democratic process is at work. The climactic issue of our time will be fought out by great blocs of organized power beyond our campuses, and for the immediate future the decision may go against the mass of the people. But over the long future, it is my belief that man will fight his way back toward more and more democracy. Meanwhile, we educators can be sure that our classrooms have a great role to play as one of the few potential active focal points for that longer future.

Robert J. Havighurst:

SOCIAL IMPLICATIONS OF THE REPORT OF THE PRESIDENT'S COMMISSION ON HIGHER EDUCATION

THE President's Commission on Higher Education has boldly stated the claim of higher education for the nation's support. The commission proposes that one half of the nation's youth should go to college for two years, instead of one sixth as at present. Furthermore, the commission says that practically all young people should complete a high-school course, instead of less than half as at present.

In order that such a large proportion of young people may go to college, the commission points out that the colleges must be changed so that they will meet the needs of students with a wider variety of expectations in life, including many who will not enter white-collar occupations. Thus it is not just "more education for more people," but more education and more appropriate education.

It is a stirring proposal. As a statement of faith in the value of education to a modern society the report will win confidence because the commission contained distinguished business and professional men as well as educators.

But what are the social implications of the expansion of education called for by the commission? What will it do to our society? And is the program feasible? Can it be made to work? These are the questions with which this paper is concerned.

Social implications. In effect, the commission recommends a two-year postponement of adulthood for all American youth. This is the meaning of extension by two years of the average educational level of the population. The policies recommended by the commission would delay the entrance of young people into the labor market, on the average, about two years. Since the average work life of a person is about 45 to 50 years, this means that the labor force would be reduced by about four per cent. Agriculture would feel this cut especially, for farm boys and girls would constitute a large proportion of the youth whose education would be lengthened.

Extension of education would also result in postponement of marriage for women, though perhaps not for men. If half of the girls in the country were to continue their education through the age of 19, and if a third of them were to continue through 21, as the commission recommends, very few of these girls would marry before 21. Yet, in 1940, 26 per cent of the nineteen-year-old women and 44 per cent of the twenty-one-year-old women were married. Unless those who married this early were mostly in

Reprinted by permission from *School and Society*, LXVII, No. 1736 (April 3, 1948), 257–261. Robert J. Havighurst is Professor of Education, University of Chicago.

the duller half of the population, and thus not fit for college in any case, it seems clear that keeping more young women in college would postpone the average age of marriage.

However, the United States is a country of early marriage — much earlier than the countries of western Europe. The average age of marriage for women is about the same in the United States as in Bulgaria. Postponement of marriage of women in the United States would tend to bring it into line with the countries of western Europe.

But delay of marriage for women might be avoided, if colleges would change their attitudes about marriage of co-eds, and permit or even encourage marriage of women students. This, however, would probably tend to reduce the age of marriage of men, which is now about three years above that of women. College women students would probably marry college men students, and men more near to their own age than is customary today.

Another social change attendant upon expansion of higher education would be an increased demand for white-collar jobs. This would result from the fact that three to four times as many people would graduate from college as in 1940. The commission considers expansion of white-collar occupations desirable, pointing to the need for more doctors, dentists, pharmacists, engineers, and teachers, and estimating that the professional, administrative, clerical, and sales occupations will expand so as to employ half again as many people as in 1940. Still, with the college expansion recommended by the commission, there would be many more college-educated people than there were professional and managerial jobs. Either these people would jam themselves into these jobs and cut the average income for people in this class, or the new college-educated group would have different occupational goals from those of the college students of today — many of them becoming industrial workers, minor clerks, and farmers. This latter outcome is expected by the commission, which urges that college courses be developed which have value as general education for people of every vocational aim and that vocational courses be developed for occupations midway on the occupational ladder.

In any case, tripling or quadrupling the proportion of college-trained people within a generation would have loud reverberations both in society at large and in the colleges themselves. During the next generation it would result in a flux of reading and recreational habits in the adult population that would keep Hollywood, the newspaper publishers, the radio producers, and the politicians on the jump to find out what the new public wanted.

Within the colleges there would be a great democratizing tendency, with the center of gravity moving from the upper-middle to the lower-middle class. Instead of the upper-middle-class values and ideology which dominate the college campuses today, lower-middle-class values and ideology would become dominant. But in the process of becoming dominant these lower-middle-class values would become modified and would probably become more like those of the upper-middle-class today.

Some colleges would resist the general trend of expansion, "general education" and "democratizing." They would become even more selective and exclusive than the exclusive colleges of today and they would look upon themselves as bulwarks of "humanism" and "intellectualism" in a college world of "materialism" and "vocationalism."

Among the definitely desirable social changes which would follow adoption of the commission's program are: (1) a better-informed citizenry on complex economic and political issues, and (2) an improvement in preparation for certain occupations of the middle level, which do not now attract college-trained people. This improvement would show in the work of medical and dental technicians, secretaries and stenographers, bank clerks and department-store salespeople, policemen and restaurant managers, who would increasingly be people with college training.

Another desirable result would be an increase of employment opportunity for older people, due to the decrease in number of young people in the labor market. The number of people over 65 will double in a generation. Many of these people are now discharged arbitrarily at a given age regardless of their working efficiency. Many of them who would rather work than rest would be able to remain in their jobs, if the competition of youth were reduced.

Feasibility of the commission's program. Turning to the question of the feasibility of the commission's program, one can discern three principal obstacles to its success. One of these, the problem of financing such a program, is put in its place by the commission with the contention that the nation cannot afford *not* to invest the necessary funds in the better citizenship and the greater productivity that the program would produce.

A second possible obstacle is the ability-level of the youth of the country. How many young people have the ability to profit from education at the college level? This question is clearly a complex one, depending partly on the type of education program offered in college. The commission handles the question well by giving evidence that half of the population have intellectual abilities as high as or higher than the ability of those who are now just able to make passing grades in the first two years of college.

The third obstacle to the realization of the commission's program has hardly been mentioned in the report. This is the problem of *motivation,* which is a *cultural* problem. Will practically all boys and girls actually want to finish high school, if given the chance, and will one half of them enter college, and will one third of them go to college for four years if they are given the opportunity? To these questions the commission gives no explicit attention, but says, "The probable shift in social attitudes toward the desirability of increased education, together with economic aid, will lead more people to complete additional years of schooling."

Consideration of the facts concerning people's attitudes toward higher education makes this prophecy of the commission appear decidedly optimistic. To be sure, there is some evidence that more young people would take advantage of increased educational opportunity should it become available. Probably the most convincing evidence of this sort is the record of two states, California and Utah, which have maintained a policy for at least two decades of increasing educational opportunity at the higher levels. In 1940 California had 41 per cent and Utah had 43 per cent of the 18- and 19-year-olds in school. The proportion of 20-year-olds in educational institutions was 20 and 21 per cent, respectively, for these two states. These figures are about midway between the national averages and the goals set by the commission. They show that substantial increases of enrollment are feasible in some states. But they also indicate that the practicable limits may be somewhat below the commission's estimates, for neither of these two states has shown much increase of school enrollment since 1930.

A more thorough study of the feasibility of the commission's program requires consideration of the distribution of *motivation* for higher education throughout the population. Do all kinds of people want their children to go to college? Or is this phenomenon pretty largely limited to people at the upper end of the socioeconomic scale? The answer is clearly that different social groups have different degrees of motivation for higher education.

The desire for college education is found as a general rule only in people at the upper end of the socioeconomic scale. It is present only in exceptional cases among people at the lower end of the scale. Whereas three fourths to nine tenths of upper-class and upper-middle-class people send their children to college, about one fifth of lower-middle-class youth go to college. But 40 per cent of the population are in the lower-middle-class and less than 10 per cent are in the upper-middle and upper classes. To be sure, economic barriers keep some lower-middle-class youths out of college, but there is evidence that lack of motivation for higher education rather than lack of money puts a stop to education of boys and girls in many lower-middle-class families. . . .

To get an accurate knowledge of the reasons why more children of the lower-middle and lower classes do not go to college, one must study these children and their families. This has been done by the writer and his colleagues in several Midwestern communities. On the basis of these studies it can be said that the motivational barrier is at least as important as the economic barrier in keeping these young people out of college.

That is, fully as many able young people fail to go to college because they lack the desire as those who fail to go to college because they lack the money. Examples of cases with varying degrees of motivation are the following:

A is a girl, now aged 16, who has been studied since she was 10 years old. She has an IQ of 130 and has been one of the three top students in her class. She is a serious-minded, rather bookish girl. Her father owns two houses and has a small civil-service job. She is the only child, and her parents could afford to send her to college. A field worker recently said to A, "What would you like to be doing when you are 21?" A replied, "Oh, I'd like to be out of school. I don't plan to finish college. I'm just going to go to school for a while and when I'm 21 I expect to be out." Here is one of the three or four ablest young people in her age group in a typical Midwestern small city. She expects to go to college, but then to drop out after a couple of years. Her motivation for college is low.

B is a young woman, now about 22, who led her class in scholarship in high school. She was a beautiful girl, attractive to boys and popular with girls. Her personality and popularity, combined with an IQ of 140, marked her as the outstanding student of her class. She was one of a large family of children with immigrant parents who lived simply and neatly in the poorest section of town. But her older brothers and sisters were earning good money and could help her get an education. Furthermore, her high-school teachers wanted to help her, and they secured offers of scholarships from two colleges. And one of them, who had received help herself in college, anonymously set up a senior scholarship of $250 to be given to B. After all this, B decided not to go to college. She took a minor clerical job in the town and stayed home with her mother.

In the same high school class as B was C, the son of a widow whose husband had been a laborer. An older unmarried daughter supported the family. C was a rather plain youth, earnest and industrious and well thought of, though not especially popular among his age-mates. He was above average in ability, with an IQ of 120, but never outstanding in scholarship. C was extremely ambitious. He once wrote in answer to the question "What is the best thing that could happen to you?" the following, "The best thing is that I should somehow get enough money and enough education to succeed in the profession I have chosen for myself." Aided by his minister and his Sunday-school teacher, C secured a scholarship to a small college. After a year he went into the army, and now with GI money he is continuing his education.

These cases illustrate the importance of motivation, as distinguished from financial support, in determining whether a young person shall go to college. The high-school seniors of the town where these three young people live were asked in 1946 to agree to or disagree with the proposition —"There is plenty of educational opportunity in America for everyone, regardless of his background." Eighty-seven per cent of these young people agreed to this statement. Yet only about 20 per cent of these young people, already a select group, expected to go to college.

Studies now under way by colleagues of the writer are seeking to discover what proportion of the young people of the lower-middle and lower classes have the drive and the motivation to finish high school and go to college. At present it is estimated that, of the upper half in scholastic ability, approximately half are motivated strongly enough to get to college, if they have financial assistance, while the other half are not sufficiently interested. If this estimate be taken as valid and as applicable throughout the United States, it is possible to estimate how many young people would go to college, if the economic barriers were removed.

Making the most optimistic assumptions — that half of all lower-middle- and lower-class youth have sufficient intellectual ability to go to college and that half of this group who are not now in college would go if they had financial assistance, we secure the figures of Table 2.

TABLE 2 — *Increased College Attendance if Economic Barriers Were Removed*

Class	Per cent of total age group	Per cent who now go to college	Additional per cent with ability and motivation	Additional per cent of total age group
Lower-middle	40	20	½ of 30=15	6
Lower	52	5	½ of 45=22.5	12
				18

An additional 18 per cent would attend college, if they had a chance, making a total of 35 per cent. This is to be compared with the commission's recommendation of 50 per cent.

If the foregoing evaluation of the motivation factor is substantially correct, the proportion of young people going to college could be doubled by increased financial assistance, but not tripled as the commission proposes.

Thus there is a problem of motivation for higher education to be overcome if the commission's goals are to be realized. To solve this problem — that is, to get more young people to *want to go to college* two things are necessary:

1. To convince working-class people and the lower levels of white-collar workers that "general education" at the college level is worth more for their children than the money they could otherwise be earning.

2. To improve the guidance processes in the high schools so as to do a better job of encouraging the ablest half of the youth population to continue into college.

The magnitude of the motivational

problem as compared with the economic problem can also be estimated if one studies the figures for high-school and college enrollments of 1947 as compared with 1940. Nineteen forty was still part of the Great Depression, with considerable unemployment and an NYA program of economic assistance to college students. The year 1947 was much better, economically, than 1940. In particular, working-class people and farmers had higher real incomes in 1947 than in 1940. They were better able to send their children to college in 1947 than in 1940. This may have been partly due to the pressure of GI enrollment, which filled some colleges so full that younger people who would normally have been admitted were turned away. But it is also partly due to the fact that jobs were more plentiful in 1947 than in 1940, and many young people took the job in preference to college. Motivation for college education was not so strong in them as motivation for earning money.

The plain fact is that the trends toward greater enrollment in the last years of high school and of college have been arrested, perhaps permanently, since 1940. It is possible that we have already reached the maximum of college and high-school enrollments. Almost certainly we have reached the maximum that is possible without either greater economic assistance to students or greater motivation for higher education on the part of young people.

Consequently, the commission's statement —"Obviously, what this commission recommends is simply an acceleration of trends in higher education as they were before World War II"— leads to an oversimplification of the situation. The prewar trend had practically run its course, and even a continuation of the trend, to say nothing of its acceleration, would require explicit effort and planning on the part of the society.

Unless something is done soon, on the economic and the motivational fronts, there will certainly be fewer college students in 1952 than in 1940, due to a decrease of 10 per cent in the population of the 18–21 age group. Colleges which are now bursting with students will have empty spaces in classrooms and dormitories.

Actually, then, a decrease rather than an increase of college enrollments is to be anticipated during the next decade unless measures are taken to increase enrollments. And the commission's goals for higher education can only be approached through a change in the cultural motivations of American lower-middle-class and working-class people, which makes them value college education more highly than they do today.

Seymour E. Harris:

MILLIONS OF B.A.'s, BUT NO JOBS

IN a bold and stimulating report, the President's Commission on Higher Education has proposed for 1960 an enrollment of 4.6 million students in American institutions of higher learning. Enrollment at the present time seems to be just about 2.5 millions and educators seem to be in agreement that universities and colleges will enroll 3 millions by the Fifties.

These are astronomical figures, which point up the rapid expansion of higher education in the United States. In 1870 our colleges graduated only 9,000 students. As late as 1900 the total enrollment in all institutions of higher learning was only 238,000. Now less than a generation and a half later we have more than ten times that number and the President's commission proposes to double the present output of college graduates within another twenty years.

This means a vast future increase in college graduates — an increase proportionately much greater than the gain in population. In 1940 the number of college graduates was nearly 4 million, or about 3 per cent of the population. At present-day enrollments we can expect at least 10 million people with college diplomas by the Nineteen Sixties.

At the rate of increase recommended by the President's commission the country would have, eighteen or twenty years from now, about 15 million graduates, or almost four times the present number.

And it is not difficult to envision a "college-bred" population of 30 millions or even 45 millions, if one counts all those who have had as much as two years of college. Indeed, if all the recommendations of the President's commission were carried out, the time would come when we would be confronted with a college-graduate population of as much as 25 to 35 per cent of the nation's labor force.

At first thought this might seem an excellent thing. It is a generally accepted proposition that educational progress is linked to social and material progress. But there are long-range implications in the commission's proposals which must be considered. One problem is of primary importance. What do college graduates expect of the world and what do they get for their education? What opportunities are open to them?

The first question is a purely vocational one, but full of social, economic and political meaning. As a college teacher for almost thirty years who has observed undergraduates at close range, I am convinced that vocational reward is still the most important consideration prodding young men and women to go to college. They accept general education in large part because the subject-matter and the process of learning make them more fit to earn a living, because a college education increasingly is a passport to the most coveted openings.

In view of this preoccupation with in-

Reprinted by permission from *New York Times Magazine* (January 2, 1949), p. 9 ff. Seymour E. Harris is Professor of Economics, Harvard University.

creased income — and with the prestige attached to brain work — it is interesting to consider the part the college graduate plays in the labor market. His place in our present economy, or rather in the economy of 1940 when the last census was taken, is indicated by figures.

Nearly all of the college graduates belonged to the proprietorship-executive-managerial and professional classes, as those are defined by the census. The first group includes a large proportion of the employes in business. The professional group includes doctors, lawyers, teachers, scientists, engineers, Government workers and employes in the newspaper, radio, advertising, entertainment and many other fields. About 70 per cent of the graduates were in the professions, most of the remainder in the proprietorship-executive-managerial class. Only about 5 per cent of the jobs in the entire labor force require or attract college graduates.

If we assume that in the Nineteen Sixties college men and women would seek the same kinds of employment and in the same proportions as in 1940, definite conclusions may be drawn. There simply would be far more graduates than jobs. Nor could we expect Government and business to take up the slack. While college graduates seem to be increasingly interested in Government positions, the Government depends mostly on non-college people for the bulk of its routine clerical tasks. And with the gradual depopulation of the farming areas and the growth of large business, the college graduate will not find many additional openings to his liking in the "executive" field.

The need for executives does not increase in proportion to the growth of population. From 1910 to 1940, while the population was increasing 36 per cent,

the number of openings for executives was increased only 8 per cent. And from 1929 to 1946 the number of active proprietors of unincorporated enterprises (roughly, the field of small business) actually declined 2.6 per cent.

If we look at the professions, the employment picture is equally dark. On the basis of the proposed increase in graduates we could expect 7 million people with college diplomas looking for jobs in the professions by the Nineteen Sixties — a horde of would-be professional workers about four times as great as the number of professional jobs filled by college graduates in 1940.

A large proportion of these, perhaps 3.5 millions, would be teachers. It seems certain that most of them would not find teaching jobs of any kind. For the country supported only one million teachers in 1940 and these so inadequately that replacements could not be assured without a general lowering of qualifications. It would require a revolution in finance to increase teaching staffs by a mere 50 per cent within the next twenty years. Even then only three-sevenths of the anticipated number of teachers would be able to find jobs in that profession.

I continue to assume that the number seeking employment in each profession is determined by the ratio of college graduates in the profession in 1940. Thus if one-half of all college graduates were teachers in 1940, then if there promises to be 10 million graduates, there would be 5 million potential teachers.

In medicine the picture is not fundamentally different, though different problems are involved. There is, of course, a shortage of doctors and dentists. The nation might well use twice as many as it has now or a total of over 400,000. But it is not clear just what would happen to the remainder of the 1.6 million young men and women who would aspire to the medical profession under the expanded program, even if the country could use 400,000.

In 1940 the nation had about 338,000 scientists. Under the commission's proposals the universities and colleges could be expected to run the total up to 942,000, including engineers, within the next twenty years. This would involve certain complications. The commission itself points out that engineers face a saturated market by 1950.

Eight years ago there were some 180,000 lawyers in the United States. It could be argued that this number would be quite enough to handle all the legal work twenty years hence. Indeed, as the Committee on the Economic Status of the Legal Profession has said, lawyers could do more preventive work and could eliminate some people who should not be giving legal advice. Yet under the expanded college program it seems reasonable to expect 860,000 people trained for the law by the Nineteen Sixties, almost five times the present number.

All these estimates are based, of course, on the assumption that college people would choose the same profession in the same ratio that they did in 1940. This would not be true in all cases. Some people would be discouraged from entering the most crowded professions. Economic conditions might keep some students out of college or govern their choice of professions.

Yet, after all allowances are made and exceptions noted, we could still expect an outpouring of college graduates into an economy which probably would not be prepared to receive them. If there are basic changes due in the economy which would eliminate the problem one cannot imagine what they are.

What would be the result of a rapidly expanding proletariat of the A.B. and the Ph.D.? Obviously any new outpouring of young hopefuls, with their special brand of aspiration and disillusionment, is of vital importance to the American economy as well as to the college graduate himself. If American colleges and universities doubled or tripled their output within the course of a generation, it would be a significant social change. The change has already begun to occur.

University graduates have been accustomed to receive certain rewards in the form of income and station. In general the college graduate and the professional worker still earn more than the non-college graduate and the non-professional. But the overflow of high school and college graduates is beginning to be felt. It is reflected in the higher pay for craftsmen than for educated clerical and kindred workers; in the relative losses of white-collar workers over the last fifty years; in lower pay for school teachers than for factory workers or tradesmen.

Lower wages may serve the purpose of crowding some professional workers — not all of them underpaid, by any means — out of their chosen professions into other jobs where they may or may not be able to capitalize on their training. Is this not merely the principle of supply and demand at work in the field of education, it may be asked? One might call it that. But there is something wrong with a principle of supply and demand which steadily produces a flow of college-trained people who cannot be accommodated in their chosen professions. If, under an expanded program of higher learning, the candidates out-numbered the jobs five or six to one, serious complications might set in.

What are the likely results? Would we be compelled to change some of our attitudes toward higher learning? Would medical societies and bar associations meet the problem by recourse to more severe restrictionism? How would a college-graduate population five times as large as in 1932 react to a severe depression and mass unemployment?

Some of the results can be anticipated. Frustration. Anti-intellectualism. The bolstering of revolutionary forces by millions of college graduates who had hoped to be executives, college teachers, physicians and lawyers. Bumper crops of new graduates thrown into an economy unprepared to absorb them would certainly bring with them a bumper crop of disillusionment. Kotschnig, in his important study of "Unemployment in the Learned Professions," showed well the contributions of the disappointed intellectuals to the rise of fascism in Europe.

What is the answer to the problem?

With a greater surplus of college graduates, many non-college men and women would undoubtedly be squeezed out of some professions, retailing and other employments. Legislatures could pass laws setting up a college degree as a requirement for certain kinds of employment. But a diploma should not serve as a passport when education does not contribute to the productivity of a profession. Too much insistence upon a college degree excludes other worthy candidates from jobs and further accelerates the stampede to college.

Inadequate facilities and restrictionism do not constitute a good defense against an overflow of professional workers. The supply and demand for professional people is a public rather than a group-interest problem, and public need does not always coincide with the self-interests of medical societies, for example. The nation spent three times as much for medicine in 1946 as it did in 1932. During this same fourteen-year period the number of doctors and dentists increased by only 5 per cent, though the rise for the economy as a whole was 55 per cent. To open the doors of the medical profession a little wider, it might be necessary to make a frontal attack on restrictionism, overhaul the financing of medicine and establish a comprehensive program of federal aid and health insurance.

Clearly there is need for a thorough study of the supply and demand for college-trained men and women. President Conant of Harvard has asked for an inventory of jobs and job-seekers. Commissioner of Education Spaulding has requested a similar survey for New York State. I have made a provisional census of the market for educated men and women. A more searching study awaits the financial support of Government or some large research organization. We are spending about 10 per cent of our national income on education. (This estimate allows for income foregone.) Perhaps it is time to spend some money trying to determine the relationship between education and the national economy.

One of the other needs is for improved publicity on the part of colleges and Government. What are the objects of a college education? What can a college graduate expect in the labor market? And just what does he expect? Perhaps many high school graduates are rushing off to college who should have stayed at home or joined the labor market.

Then again our traditional attitudes toward higher learning may need to be re-examined. We profess to believe in higher learning for its own sake. Yet we expect a college degree to pay cash dividends, to open up greater economic opportunities. Perhaps we overstress the vocational gains.

It may be that we should stop putting so much emphasis in our own minds on the monetary value of a college education and put more emphasis on the intangible social and cultural values to be derived from learning. The time may be coming when we will have to start accepting the idea that education is life, not merely a preparation for it. As John Dewey put it, "Living has its own intrinsic quality and the business of education is with that quality." In any case, the graduates of the next generation will have to find more and more justification for their college education on other than economic grounds.

In the meantime it is up to college administrators and to the Government to clarify the situation. The boy or girl preparing for college has a right to know what to expect.

Algo D. Henderson: THE MARKET FOR COLLEGE GRADUATES – A REVIEW

IN his recent book, *The Market for College Graduates,* Dr. Seymour E. Harris has explored a topic of serious importance and interest.

The record shows that there has been a steady increase over the past 50 years or more in the number of students attending and being graduated from college. Predictions have been made by numerous educators and educational commissions that this trend will continue. For various reasons it seems probable that the number of college students ten to fifteen years from now will be at least 25% greater than it is at present, and it is possible that it will be considerably higher. This raises the serious question, What occupations will be open to college graduates when their numbers become so large? It is this phase of the subject of college education that Dr. Harris has analyzed in great detail.

His is not wholly a theoretical or speculative analysis. His book has been documented voluminously. We are indebted to Dr. Harris for his expert presentation of facts relating to the labor market for college graduates. It is good to see an economist who is an authority in his field apply his knowledge and skill to the economics of higher education.

The approach of Dr. Harris is that of analyzing the possible future careers of college graduates from the viewpoint of the traditional occupations into which college students have been going in the past. This is, of course, a logical approach and brings sharply into focus the problems relating to the purposes of higher education and the kinds of occupational careers for which colleges prepare their students.

Although the book makes a valuable contribution to the discussion of this one

Reprinted by permission from *Harvard Educational Review,* XX, No. 2 (Spring, 1950), 112–121. Dr. Henderson, Associate Commissioner of Education, State of New York, and formerly President of Antioch College, was a member of the President's Commission.

phase of the subject of college education, it is not a wholly satisfying book in certain respects. Dr. Harris has presented his data in such detail as to obscure somewhat the constructive conclusions of the book — phases of the subject which need much additional consideration. One of the issues raised is this question: At this stage of the development of our democratic society is it a sound assumption that college youth should be educated primarily for certain prestige occupations and professions? Or should the occupational outlet for college graduates be much broader than that? A second issue also arises because of the nature of the democratic society which we in the United States are evolving. Is the function of college education primarily pre-professional or professional — that is, occupational — or is the primary function that of educating broadly an increasingly large portion of the total population?

If the assumption is correct that students and their parents, and also the presidents and faculties of our colleges, think of college education primarily in relation to training for the more traditional professions, it becomes a matter of crucial importance that the colleges reconsider their objectives and that they exert strong leadership toward redirecting the thinking of the American people about the aims and values of college education.

The Impact of Numbers

The estimates of future college enrollments all agree, allowing for some possible decline during the period from 1950 to 1957, that there will be a still further increase in numbers. The birth rate of the war and postwar years alone will bring a substantial increase in the number of students in college in and after 1958, assuming only that the percentage of youth attending college remains the same. The number of children born during the five years ending in 1947 was 33% more than the number born in the last five prewar years. Further gains are to be expected because the percentage of youth attending college has been steadily increasing. There is no reason to suppose that there will be a change in this trend. One reliable indication of this expectation is that where communities and states have provided educational facilities beyond the high school that are readily accessible to young people the enrollments have increased to double and more than double the numbers attending college in other areas. Another substantiating factor is the rapidly increasing percentage of youth who have been graduated from high school and thus have become eligible for possible admission to college.

The inventory of talent taken by the President's Commission on Higher Education indicated that there were four million youth who had sufficient intellectual ability to undertake satisfactory work either in a two-year or four-year program on the post-secondary level. The Commission estimated that if that many undergraduate students should enroll in college the number of students on the graduate level might increase to a total of six hundred thousand, thus making a total possible college enrollment of 4,-600,000. Dr. Harris quotes other estimates, some of them higher than this figure and others somewhat lower. For purposes of his analysis it does not matter so much which one of the estimates is believed to be most reliable. Even the more moderate of them predict total numbers of college students of a size that would create congestion in the professions if the college programs continue to educate primarily for the traditional professions. Indeed there are some fields (as in medicine) in which the pressure of students demanding admission now far exceeds the capacity of the institutions to enroll the students.

The heart of Dr. Harris' argument is this, "Assuming an enrollment of 2.5 million, a total corresponding roughly to that of 1948, the number of active college graduates in 1968 would be 10.6 million; on an assumed enrollment of 3.2 million the number would be 12.6 million; and on the Commission's proposal of 4.6 million . . . it would be 14.5 million. Once the entire population has profited from a ratio of one to two of relevant age in junior colleges and one to three in the junior and senior years, as proposed by the President's Commission, then of a peak population of 160 million, there would be 50 million (40% of the relevant population) with the equivalent of a junior college education, 30 million (about 26%–27% of 114 million 20 years old and over in 1970) with a college education, and 16 million (15% of the relevant population) with a higher degree. These are indeed astronomical figures." Assuming possible college enrollments of 2.5 to 4.6 million by 1968 and assuming that the graduates go proportionately into the same occupations into which they were going in 1940, the percentage increase in the number of openings required in various fields would be approximately as follows: in science, 204 to 279%; in law, 353 to 483%; in the ministry, 151 to 207%; in government, 393 to 537%. In 1940, according to Dr. Harris, there were 180,000 lawyers who were practicing. By 1968 consistent with the above thesis the number of practitioners in law would have to be increased to between 636,000 and 870,000 in order to absorb the flow of students trained in law. In medicine it would take from five to seven times the number of openings that there were in

1940. Dr. Harris says that he sees "no easy remedy for the surfeit of college graduates."

In considering the effect of having so many college graduates who would be prepared for professions where there would be no adequate outlet for their energies Dr. Harris refers to the well-known work of W. M. Kotschnig, who came to the opinion that the Nazi movement in Germany was nourished to a considerable extent by the *maladjusted ideas* and energies of frustrated university graduates.[1] Kotschnig said, "In Germany the 40,000 or 50,000 workless university graduates in 1931–3 became, together with the unemployed subalterns of the old imperial army, the spearhead of the nationalist-socialist movement." Dr. Harris points out that the "European experience is a warning of the even greater dangers for the United States because of the far greater numbers in our institutions of higher learning."

Although one might question the application of Kotschnig's theory to the United States, where the whole psychology of the individual's relationship to his society is fundamentally different than has been the psychology of the German, there can be no doubt of the danger to the stability of any society where there are present large numbers of intellectually inclined persons whose individual plans and ambitions have been frustrated.

The Economic Effects of College Education

The main burden of Dr. Harris' argument relates to the economic effects in this country of producing so large a number of persons with a college education. One of his theses is that the attractive professions are no longer as attractive

[1] Walter M. Kotschnig, *Unemployment in the Learned Professions*. London, 1937.

economically as they have been. This does not mean that professional people on the whole are not getting satisfactory incomes. Physicians, for example, — where Dr. Harris charges there are restrictive controls on the number of practitioners — are currently receiving markedly higher incomes than they ever have earned in the past. The incomes of engineers, of accountants, of nurses and even of teachers have been rising; but the increases have not been nearly so rapid as have been the increases in the incomes of persons employed in non-professional categories. Wage-earners in industry, for example, have benefited much more percentage-wise than have professional people. It is not entirely clear whether these differentials are merely the result of the time lag that is characteristic of the incomes of middle-class persons during inflationary periods. To get a true picture of the relative positions of professional and non-professional persons would require averaging their incomes over the whole period of a business cycle. However, there can be no doubt of the validity of Dr. Harris' point: if in any profession the number of practitioners suddenly is increased tremendously, the incomes that can be earned by each of them will decline seriously.

There is, of course, the question whether the persistent decline of income may not automatically check the flow of young persons into the particular profession. It seems probable after a certain point of disadvantage in income has been reached that young people will become aware of the disadvantage and begin to search out programs of education that would prepare them for other fields. The history of the enrollment in colleges of veterinary medicine is a good example. Just a few years ago when horses were still being widely used, the colleges of veterinary medicine had full enrollments. When the horse was displaced by the tractor (in the late 1920's and early 30's) the enrollment in these colleges declined sharply; indeed some of the colleges were left with only a handful of students. Then, the dairy and poultry industries were placed on a more scientific basis and began to develop rapidly. Individual cows became so valuable that the farmer had to give them almost the same medical and nutritional care as he did a member of his family. Other new developments such as artificial insemination required the services of doctors of veterinary medicine. In addition, cats and dogs as family pets emerged to a higher plane of living and the slightest illness required the services of a doctor. So today we see the phenomenon of a tremendous pressure for admission on the colleges of veterinary medicine and the number of colleges has recently been increased from ten to seventeen.

Statistics prove that in the past college education has paid. College graduates definitely have had higher average incomes than have noncollege persons. Dr. Harris makes much of this point; but the economic incentive is not by any means universal among the professions. In some instances, the personnel pay little attention to the economic advantage. The ministry pays a mere pittance. Teachers seem always to be paid less than most other workers. Archeologists certainly do not get rich from the monetary standpoint. One may well question whether economic advantage is, or at least needs to be, a primary incentive to persons whose interests lead them to secure the advantages of a college education.

The author makes a careful analysis of the economic displacements in our society caused by withdrawals from the labor markets. When individuals prolong their periods of schooling obviously an equivalent portion of their time is withheld from the labor market. On the other hand, to the extent that they have acquired greater skills and thus can help to produce a greater amount of wealth (whether or not they receive a good income for themselves) the economic increment for society may be greater by reason of the period in college than it would have been if they had refrained from going to college.

It is worth making the point at this place that one of the strongest arguments that has been advanced in favor of extending free public education to include the thirteenth and fourteenth years of school, the junior college level, is to assure opportunity to youth of ages 18 and 19 to be constructively busy in improving themselves, especially during periods of slack business activity. One of the tragedies of the last depression period, excepting as the condition was alleviated through the CCC and NYA programs, was that youth of these ages became a floating population, idle and restive. It is the idle persons who have not been broadly educated that provide fertile soil for totalitarian ideas.

Broadened Occupational Outlets

It is apparent from the preceding review of Dr. Harris' material that he has pointed to a grave problem in relation to college education. We simply cannot continue to think of college education as preparing students for work in a limited number of professional outlets. We cannot continue to think of a college education as being primarily pre-professional or professional in its curriculum unless we are willing to broaden considerably our concept of what constitutes a profession. We must deflate the notion that only a few avenues for earning a living

have high prestige value and that others do not. We must cease to think largely in terms of economic advantage in one occupation relative to others and educate ourselves to think rather in terms of the variety of compensations and the different qualitative satisfactions that come to an individual who devotes his life to any particular line of activity.

Technically Dr. Harris has treated his subject satisfactorily because he is talking only about a portion of the total college population — the graduates of four-year and advanced programs. However, one of the most interesting developments of the past three decades has been the rapid growth and the diversification of curricula in technological fields in the two years following high school. The junior college is a product of this century. Already there are approximately 600 such institutions and the total enrollment is now in excess of one-half million. The character of the program, too, has been changed profoundly. No longer is the program limited to the first two years of a liberal arts course. Instead, most of the students take a combined curriculum in technical and general education. The major subjects for concentration of study vocational in type have sprouted in an ever-widening circle of occupational outlets. In general these outlets are in the sub-professions.

Studies, such as "The Guide to the Development of Programs for the Institutes of Applied Arts and Sciences" in New York State, have been made which demonstrate the demand that exists for persons trained for the sub-professions. Mechanical, electrical, tool, metallurgical and textile technologists, medical secretaries, dairy bacteriologists and retail distribution specialists are examples. It has been demonstrated that a professional engineer can make good use of approximately six individuals who have had part of his technical training. It has been argued by some leaders in the field of dentistry that if each dentist would accustom himself to using one or two dental technicians he could double the number of patients he could serve and reduce the cost of services to each. The period of war, when it was necessary to utilize our manpower to the full, demonstrated the insufficiency in the number and types of available technicians.

It may be that considerable numbers of the students who have dropped by the wayside in the usual four-year curriculum should not have been enrolled there in the first place. With adequate counseling programs their interests might have been directed into the more definitely sub-professional fields where from one to three years of college education would suffice. One of the large wastes in the college field is the time spent on the professional training of persons who do not follow their programs to a conclusion. With an ever-increasing number of students entering the colleges it becomes more and more essential that the colleges maintain adequate counseling services.

Another factor that must be taken into account is that large numbers of persons who prepare for a given field do not remain employed in that field. This is particularly characteristic of persons educated in engineering, business and the law. Figures concerning the transfer from these occupations are none too reliable but estimates have been made that 40% or more of persons educated in the law or in engineering do not remain in these professions. Education in these fields apparently has a large measure of transfer value. It is difficult therefore to make a nose count of the number of prospective graduates and come to the conclusion on the basis of these numbers that

a considerable portion of them will never be employed. A person educated in the law may be employed in one of hundreds of occupations and may be happy in his employment.

One of the changes that we must make in our thinking is with respect to what constitutes a profession. Not so long ago there were only three major professions: law, ministry and medicine. Today a typical university will have from one dozen to two dozen professional schools, but still the number of professional categories is limited. This does not necessarily mean that within any given profession the range of occupational opportunity is limited. The graduates of some of the professional schools, engineering or business administration, for example, have a wide variety of interesting outlets within the field from which to choose.

The reference to business administration reminds one of the tremendous growth which at intervals has occurred in new areas of the curriculum. In the latter half of the nineteenth century, schools of agriculture and of engineering were the fashion. Not only were forty-eight land grant colleges and universities founded but many independent schools of engineering were established. In a similar manner during the period following the first World War there was a rapid multiplication in the number of business schools, of special schools of education, schools of social work, and schools of public administration. Furthermore, their enrollments grew by leaps and bounds. Aside from the worst of the depression years there is no evidence that this great outpouring of college graduates in these new fields was greater than the demand for the services of the individuals.

It is always difficult at any given time to foresee new developments in occupational fields. It is fairly clear, however, that opportunity is now being found in at least several relatively new professions. In labor relations, for example, there is a rapid increase in the outlets for personnel officers, labor organizers and leaders, and labor arbitrators and mediators. There is evidence of a rapidly growing need on the part of labor organizations for college trained persons. At first they are used principally as staff employees in such occupations as writing, editing and statistical and other research; but organized labor has a dearth of members well qualified by education to assume responsibility within its own organizations and responsibilities of the civic and public types. If labor is to have an increasing voice in domestic affairs in this country it will be essential that large numbers of the members prepare themselves to accept high positions in government, on boards of trustees of educational, civic and philanthropical organizations and of leadership in community activities.

Other examples of relatively new professional fields are teaching on the nursery school level, clinical psychology and psychiatry, the civil service in international relations and all phases of international affairs and the organized group research required in an atomic age.

The only safe conclusion to draw from this reasoning is that American society is dynamic in nature. There is no visible reason why we need to think now that a time has been reached when conditions will remain relatively static. Discoveries for the application of atomic energy alone may tremendously accelerate the dynamic developments in our life.

We also need to remind ourselves that educating people does not increase the number of persons. Temporarily, as Dr. Harris points out, the person getting an education is actually withdrawn from the labor market. The effect of education is not to increase the number of people but to increase the ability of the individual. It also increases his versatility, a great advantage in our society based so largely upon individualism.

From this point of view a farmer becomes a better farmer if he has some education about farming that extends beyond his apprenticeship experience or his high school course in agriculture. A stenographer or secretary ordinarily can do her job more intelligently if she has had the intellectual stimulation and has achieved the broader knowledge that comes from post–high school education. Although not all clerks in government need to have a college education in order to satisfy the minimum civil service requirements one can conceive that governmental service would be superior to the present standard if the clerks had some college education. In California 50% of the professional nurses have had in addition to their technical training one or more years of college. In the Eastern states only 10% of the nurses have had this amount of education. One would assume that California has better nurses because of the greater understanding they probably have gained of the patient's intellectual, psychological and emotional welfare by reason of having had the additional college training.

The Function of College Education

Although the farmer becomes a better farmer by reason of his college education, the value of his education is not limited to the vocational aspect of his life. He may also lead a better life by reason of the wider understanding he has achieved respecting the world in which he lives. The satisfaction he gains from the use of his leisure may have been improved. If these things are true for the farmer, they are also true for the carpenter, the bank teller and the arc welder. Perhaps this phase of the subject can be understood most clearly if the college education of women is considered. The large majority of women get married and most of these do not continue in an occupation outside of the home. This is as true of college women as of others. Assuming that most college women become homemakers, does this imply that they need not or should not have gone to college? Or has college been the means of giving them other satisfactions in living and helped them in many intangible ways to make a better home for husband and children? Many of these women, too, become the strongest civic workers and community leaders.

The demand for college education undoubtedly bears some relationship to the standard of living in a country. The production of college graduates in turn must be one of the means of raising the level of the standard of living. There exist, in the world, countries with large natural resources and much greater population than has the United States and yet their standards of living are much lower. It is reasonable to suppose that the American standard of living will continue to improve, and certainly it will with respect to the extension of more of the benefits to a larger portion of the population. This is one reason why there is a persistent increase in the demand for college education. Education is one of the satisfactions in living to be had when people can afford it.

There is still another factor that argues for more rather than less college education. An educator who was trained on the continent and had spent a few years in England at the beginning of the last war remarked that he thought the reason England was unable to get under way as quickly in its mobilization for war as did

the United States later was that England had failed to provide sufficiently for the education of her people. For large portions of the population she had depended upon apprenticeship training to produce knowledge and skills for work. One of the results was an inability to convert quickly and easily her machine processes. This is a task for technically trained people. This educator thought that the land grant system of colleges and universities in this country, which had created a huge reservoir of engineers, was the significant factor that enabled American industry to forge ahead so rapidly and in wartime to adapt itself so quickly to changed conditions.

Unless it develops fully its human resources, the United States, competitively speaking, may be at some disadvantage in the future with the Eastern nations that have huge natural resources and much larger manpower. Under totalitarian governments manpower can be mobilized in a manner to make use of the resources. The advantage that the West has, in addition to its head start, is the resourcefulness, the intellectual agility and the creative ability of its people. This advantage arises through the education, especially the higher education, of people.

Presumably college education has the function of cultivating the intellectual ability of people and of bringing to them much greater knowledge and skills. In keeping with American tradition these individuals are better prepared by reason of their college training to initiate, to organize, to produce. A democracy should not be dependent upon a given clique of "leaders" who through intuition or political maneuvering determine the productive activities of a country and the kinds of lives people shall live. Neither should a democracy depend upon a small intellectual aristocracy. A democratic nation needs countless thousands and hundreds of thousands of people capable of originating ideas, projecting courses of action and administering productive group efforts. Education can provide individuals with more varied interests and greater versatility in using their talents. It can provide an orientation with respect to good living. Both versatility in occupational interests and training and a philosophical orientation to our complex life as a democratic society can help people to secure greater satisfactions from their productive efforts.

From the viewpoint of society a democracy needs an educated citizenry. The individual citizen is a voter. The government is founded upon his ballot. Our modern world is producing greatly more complex problems for the citizen to consider. They are problems relating to the humanities, the social sciences, the physical sciences. The problems no longer confine themselves to the environment of the immediate community. The citizen of today must be alert to events and trends throughout his country and throughout the world. It takes a considerable background of education today to perform well the duties of citizenship.

One of the objectives in a democracy should be to keep the way open and make it possible for each individual, within his ability, to grow in personality and to lead a full life. A recent study by the Elmo Roper Organization shows that a large percentage of parents would like their children to have the advantages of college. The craving for additional education exists. It is salutary to find this further awakening of interest in educa-tion beyond the high school. Even though these parents may be thinking primarily in terms of better occupational outlets for their children, as Roper indicates, the fact that the children get into college provides the opportunity for the educational institutions to extend the range of their cultural interests and knowledge. The next generation then will have still further capacity to absorb cultural values and increase its standard of living. Thus, upon the material base which this nation has built so well there can be founded an ever-evolving cultural life which brings within its fold all the people of the country.

Vocational and liberal education need to be intertwined in our curriculums. There has been a tendency to segregate them. There has been some tendency to adulterate the cultural programs with too much emphasis on vocational matters. Everyone needs occupational training but this part of his education needs to be in proper proportion to the total of his education. Culture is the framework within which the occupation lies. As Dr. Horace Kallen has recently said: "The root of culture is vocation; the fruit of vocation is culture."

Dr. Harris' book may be cited to prove that we do not need more college educated people in the United States. In my opinion, that would be an unfortunate conclusion to draw from the facts he presents.

The real conclusion to his analysis, which he recognizes, is that we must re-examine the purposes of education and must also redirect the thinking of people with respect to the values to be obtained from attendance at college.

Robert M. Hutchins:

DOUBLE TROUBLE: ARE MORE STUDIES, MORE FACILITIES, MORE MONEY THE KEY FOR BETTER EDUCATION?

THE Report of the President's Commission on Higher Education reflects the educational system with which it deals. It is big and booming. It is confused, confusing, and contradictory. It has something for everybody. It is generous, ignoble, bold, timid, naive, and optimistic. It is filled with the spirit of universal brotherhood and the sense of American superiority. It has great faith in money. It has great faith in courses. It is antihumanistic and anti-intellectual. It is confident that vices can be turned into virtues by making them larger. Its heart is in the right place; its head does not work very well.

Every cliché and every slogan of contemporary educational discussion appear once more. Much of the report reads like a Fourth-of-July oration in pedaguese. It skirts the edge of illiteracy, and sometimes falls over the brink. And, when the battle has ended, the field is strewn with the corpses of the straw men the Commission has slain.

The cry is "more": more money, more buildings, more professors, more students, more everything. The educational system is taken as given. It may be wasteful and shoddy. But let us expand it, even if that means that it will be more wasteful and shoddier, and all will be well.

If the Commission's purpose was to write a propaganda document, to praise American education and not to criticize it, the result is unconvincing. A good propaganda document should not promise what is obviously impossible and undesirable, as the Commission does when it proposes to double the output of doctors by 1960 and to double the staff of colleges by 1952. Only disillusionment can follow from a program which undertakes to make the American people intelligent, prosperous, and happy by the simple process of doubling the students, the professors, and the expenditures of higher educational institutions.

II

The Commission is right about many things. It is right in pointing out that higher education in the United States is free only in the sense that public colleges and universities charge low fees or none. Higher education is not free in the sense that students without money can avail themselves of it. The cost of living and the loss of earning power to their families prevent many young people from going to a free college. They are just as well qualified as those who go. Many of those who go do so because they can afford it. Many of those who do not go don't be-

Reprinted by permission from *Educational Record*, XXIX, No. 2 (April, 1948), 107–122. This article was reprinted in the *Saturday Review of Literature*, July 17, 1948, under the title that is here used. Robert M. Hutchins is Associate Director of the Ford Foundation.

cause they can't. The Commission properly insists that the economic condition of a young person's parents should not determine his educational opportunities.

The Commission sees that the economic barriers to educational opportunity must be broken down by the federal government. Only the federal government has the money. Only the federal government can equalize educational opportunity among the states. Federal equalization without federal control can best be obtained by national scholarships and fellowships; students could use them to pay their way at any accredited institution, public or private.

The Commission attacks the economic barriers to education by advocating the wide extension of the junior college movement. These institutions, which the Commission prefers to call "community colleges," enable the student to live at home through the conventional sophomore year. The Commission favors making this college as free to the student as the high school is today. Although, as we shall see, the Commission has no clear idea of the purpose, organization, or activities of the community college, the Commission does understand that this unit can do much to equalize educational opportunity.

The Commission strongly condemns those barriers to educational opportunity which have been thrown up by racial and religious prejudice. These are indefensible, and have never been defended on their merits. The defense has been that colleges and universities would do more harm than good, or at least would do no good, to those whom they were trying to help, if they took a stand against discrimination which was much in advance of the communities in which they were located. Actually the horrid consequences predicted when the removal of discrimination is discussed in educational institutions never materialize when it is removed. If there were some unpleasantness, it could not be regarded as important. What is important is that institutions of higher learning should stand for something. If they will not stand for the Rights of Man, how can they expect anybody else to?

The Commission is on sound ground when it urges the extension of the educational opportunities open to adults. Many adults have had no education, including great numbers who have graduated from college. Education is a process which should go on through the whole of life. Many disciplines, and they are among the most important, will not give up their secrets except to those who have had experience with the issues which the disciplines raise. The education of youth is a waste of time if youth is to have no future. Unless we can educate those who control the world today, it seems most unlikely that youth can have a future.

The Commission is right on many other matters with which it deals more briefly. It is right on the value of technical aids to learning, though it exaggerates the educational possibilities of AM broadcasting. It is right on the place of intercollegiate athletics. It rightly attacks specialization, the narrow preparation of college teachers, and the limitations which professions place on their numbers in order to increase the prestige or value of their services. It rightly urges the support of basic research by industry, though it says, for reasons which are obscure, that half the support of basic research must in the future come from the federal government. It opposes secrecy in research and the control of research by the military. It is for academic freedom.

III

It is impossible to form a judgment on some sections of the report, because it is impossible to discover what the Commission's attitude is. The most important of the issues which the Commission leaves unresolved is that of the organization of education. Yet, unless this question can be intelligently settled, the extension of the junior colleges will be of doubtful benefit to the country; much of the money which the Commission wishes to have spent on education will be wasted; and the system which results will be inferior to the one we have today.

Apparently because it does not wish to arouse the antagonism of vested interests, the Commission dodges the question of organization every time the question rears its head. The Commission does so even when its arguments seem to lead inevitably to an attack on the problem and a rational solution of it. The Commission says (III, 7), "The senior high school and the first two years of college, particularly the liberal arts college, are similar in purpose, and there is much duplication of content in their courses." It goes on (III, 12), "The present difficulty grows largely out of the fact that the academic work of the last 2 years of the high school and that of the first 2 years of the typical arts college are essentially identical in purpose." We then find (III, 17) that "Many young people of ages 16, 17, 18, and 19 are well suited for residence on a college campus. In the school system developed on the 6–4–4 plan, the last unit embraces these ages. Liberal arts colleges may well parallel this last unit. . . . Furthermore there is a tendency at present to stretch out too long the period of pre-professional and professional study. Students ought much more generally than now to enter many fields of professional study

when not older than 20. . . . Today the age of 20 falls in the middle of the arts college course." Later the Commission says (III, 70) in urging a great increase in the number of community colleges, "This development should be guided by a State-wide plan in which at least the following features should be found: (1) The larger municipalities will extend their public school programs to include the thirteenth and fourteenth years or grades, thus making possible further experimentation with the 6–4–4 plan."

Meanwhile we have learned (III, 18) that, "The present plan of building a curriculum for a bachelor's degree and then another often poorly related program for a master's degree is far inferior as a preparation for teaching than would be a unified 3-year program above the community college, or above the sophomore year of the liberal arts college."

From these quotations one might suppose that the Commission, recognizing the waste and incoherence of two-year units and two-year courses of study, would recommend a six-year elementary school, a four-year high school, a four-year college, and a three-year program to the master's degree. One might even suppose that the Commission would be forced to suggest the relocation or elimination of the bachelor's degree, since that degree obviously interferes with the construction of an intelligible curriculum to the master's. The Commission does none of these things. It assumes that the bachelor's degree must stay where it is. In general it assumes an 8–4–2–2–1 program to the master's; its pages are studded with references to "2-year curricula" in the senior high school, the junior college, and the senior college. We even hear (III, 5) that, "The two-year college — that is the thirteenth and fourteenth years of our educational system — is about as widely needed today as the 4-year high school was a few decades ago."

Far from being widely needed, the two-year college disrupts the educational system. As the Commission shows, it duplicates the high school; it cuts the college of liberal arts in half and makes it a two-year unit, too. The opportunity which the Commission had, and missed, was the opportunity to follow its own reasoning to the creation of a 6-4-4-3 system to the master's degree and to put the bachelor's degree, two-year units, and two-year curriculums, with the inefficiency, duplication, and aimlessness which they reflect and cause, to sleep forever.

IV

Some difficulties arise in discussing matters even more important than the organization of education because the Commission, through inadvertence, indecision, or a desire to please everybody, contradicts or qualifies its statements to such an extent that it is possible to prove almost anything from the report.

For example, we are told at the outset (I, 6) that "to assume that all we need to do is apply to present and future problems 'eternal' truths revealed in earlier ages is likely to stifle creative imagination and intellectual daring." A few pages farther on (I, 11–12) we learn that, "The everlasting moral essence of democracy lies in its fundamental principles, not in its means and methods of the moment."

The Commission appears indifferent to all considerations of quality in education; but it says (I, 44), "Simply to keep more of our youth in school for a longer period will not of itself, of course, achieve the personal and social ends we have in

mind. The measure to which extended educational opportunities accomplish our purposes will depend on the kind of education provided."

The Commission seems to think that education should be infinitely diversified; but it says (I, 46), "Yet in the midst of all the necessary diversity we must somehow preserve and expand a central unity. We must make sure that every student includes the kind of learning and experience that is essential to fit free men to live in a free society."

These contradictions and qualifications illustrate one of the fundamental misconceptions upon which the report is based. This is the assumption that education can do everything and that education ought to do everything. Since education can do everything and ought to do everything, it can and should pursue conflicting purposes, for every purpose is as good as every other. Hence there can be no such thing as a contradiction in the report. I am reminded of a great educator I once knew who, when he was told that something he proposed was wrong and that he ought to do the opposite, would say, "We'll do that too!"

The fact that distresses the Commission most is that in 1945 half the children of America were growing up in families which had a cash income of $2,530 or less. The Commission is pained to learn that the birth rate is highest in the families with the lowest income. When we get to the second volume of the report (II, 11), we find the Commission saying in passing that, "All measures which will contribute to increasing the total national productivity thus become essential as indirect means toward lessening economic barriers to education." But the whole report is based upon the proposition that it is necessary to overcome the maldistribution in income by expenditures on education itself.

If the economic barriers to education arise because of the inequities in the economic system, and if the birth rate is highest in the families with the lowest incomes, the first consideration of the educational statesman should be to remove the inequities in the economic system and to raise the income or lower the birth rate of the families with the lowest incomes and the highest birth rate. The Commission is a little sanctimonious about the birth rate. It says (I, 32), "No one would suggest that the proper remedy for this situation is a lower birth rate in any part of the country." But if we can raise the incomes of the families with the lowest incomes, we shall lower the birth rate of those families and hence lower the birth rate in the parts of the country in which those families live.

It may be said that there is no harm in the fact that the Commission takes the economic system for granted and tries to see what can be done to overcome the handicaps which it causes by direct assistance to students and institutions: the Commission was appointed to study education and not economics. The reply is that the Commission gives its powerful support to the omnibus fallacy, the doctrine that education, more education, more expensive education, will solve every problem and answer every prayer. The omnibus fallacy diverts the public mind from direct attack on the evil under consideration by proposing the easy, if costly, alternative, "Let education do it." In the case of the economic barriers to education it is clear that whatever is done by way of scholarship or grants-in-aid to institutions cannot go to the heart of the matter. But our people are likely to think that, if they make the vast educational expenditures recommended by the Commission, the problem is solved.

V

According to the omnibus fallacy there is nothing which education cannot do; and it can do everything equally well. Education, in this view, cannot decline a task because it is not qualified to perform it; education cannot suggest that another agency or institution could perform it better. In discussing the kind of higher education it wants, the Commission gets more and more inclusive until its summary "sentence" is this (II, 6), "One which is not only general and liberal, not only sufficiently vocational, not only for broad competence in citizenship and in the wise use of leisure, but also an integrated and meaningful combination of all these aims at successive levels of education in accordance with the potentialities of each.". . .

Education cannot do everything. It cannot do everything equally well. It cannot do some things as well as other social institutions can do them or could do them if these institutions were forced to discharge their responsibilities instead of leaving the educational system to struggle along with them by default. It may be that education could teach our people to build richly textured and gracious lives if it were free to concentrate on that task. It may be that our people can learn to make a living without asking higher education to teach them how. It seems altogether likely that the attempt on the part of education to do what it cannot do well will prevent it from doing what it can do well. One of the things education cannot do well is vocational training. That can best be conducted on the job. The rapid changes in technology and the mobility of our population make vocational training given one day in one place a handicap the next day in another place. "Rarely does a college student expect necessarily to live in the State where he is attending college."

VI

Among the objectives of general education the Commission lists certain "basic outcomes." The student must be taught to be healthy: "What is needed is a course . . ." (I, 54). The student must be taught the knowledge and attitudes basic to a satisfying family life: "Such a general course would include . . ." (I, 56). The student must be taught to "get on well with people" (I, 53). The picture is one of the student coming to the college absolutely naked, with no past, no parents, no church, even without any Boy Scouts, being carefully swathed in layers of courses and sent out into the world, ready to cope with any economic, political, domestic, social, or meteorological vicissitudes. I say it cannot be done; and I say that, if it is attempted, the educational system will fail in the attempt, and, what is more important, it will fail in its proper task.

The Commission at the end of its list of eleven basic outcomes (How can an outcome be basic? And can eleven outcomes all be equally basic?) says, "Ability to think and to reason, within the limits set by one's mental capacity, should be the distinguishing mark of an educated person" (I, 57). With this I entirely agree. The distinguishing mark of the educated person is intellectual power. Hence, the primary aim of higher education is the development of intellectual power. Any other aim is secondary and can be tolerated only to the extent to which the attempt to achieve it does not interfere with the effort to achieve the primary aim. Such an aim as adjustment to the environment is not merely secondary,

it is wrong: it would prevent education from putting forth its noblest effort, the effort to produce men like Socrates and Gandhi, who were not adjusted to their environment, who did not "get on well with people," and who died because they did not.

Although one would think that the proper task of higher education was to place the distinguishing mark of the educated person, intellectual power, upon those who pass through our colleges and universities, the Commission never misses a chance to communicate the news that our educational institutions are far too intellectual. This will certainly surprise the students, parents, administrators, and citizens who have had anything to do with our educational system. To the disinterested observer the American educational system looks like a gigantic playroom, designed to keep the young out of worse places until they can go to work.

The Commission solemnly warns the colleges and universities not to turn out a generation of impractical visionaries. Oh, for just one impractical visionary a year! The Commission deplores "the present orientation of higher education towards verbal skills and intellectual interests" (I, 32). It says that American schools and colleges are preoccupied with the training of the intellect. It even thinks that faculty meetings are too intellectual and recommends "deliberations which have some immediate results, such as the purchase of new movie projectors, or the issuance of a career guidebook for students" (IV, 40). It urges administrators to be irrational. "Administrators tend to think in terms of a logical approach to curriculum problems — formulating an over-all philosophy first, then stating broad objectives, appraising the present program in terms of those objectives, defining weaknesses, and discovering ways to eliminate them. Experience demonstrates that this approach is likely to be unproductive of the one essential change, a change in the thinking and teaching and research activities of individual faculty members" (IV, 41). And so we end up with a college in which neither the students, the faculty, nor the officers are supposed to think, or, at least, to look as though they were thinking.

VII

The report calls again and again for greater diversification in education. It says, "There is already a wide variety of purposes and programs in American colleges . . ." (This would appear to be an understatement.) ". . . but there is need for even greater diversification and experimentation to take account of different kinds and degrees of intellectual capacity, talent, and interest" (II, 7). The Commission believes that, "As we bring more and more students to the campus, we shall increase in proportion the tremendous variety of human and social needs the college programs must meet. We shall add to the already overwhelming diversity of aptitudes, interests, and levels of attainment that characterize the student body. And so we shall have to increase the diversification of curricular offerings and of teaching methods and materials to correspond" (I, 45–46).

Since American institutions of higher education are already so diversified that neither the faculty nor the students can talk with one another except about the weather, politics, and last Saturday's game, the Commission's advice is a little like telling a drowning man that he can improve his position by drinking a great deal of water. On the very next page the Commission says, in bold-face type, that the colleges are failing in large part "because the unity of liberal education has been splintered by overspecialization" (I, 47). This is one time when the Commis-

sion cannot have it both ways: either it must admit that it does not care about liberal education, or it must recognize that it is impossible to offer a program that includes everything that might interest everybody, from acrobatics to zymurgy, and have it add up to a liberal education. If you believe, as the Commission says it does, in bold-face type (I, 49), that, "The crucial task of higher education today, therefore, is to provide a unified general education for American youth," then you must find out what that education is; you must offer it to American youth; and you must not divert your mind or theirs from this crucial task until you are sure that it has been accomplished.

The Commission's program of infinite diversification rests on a non sequitur. Since men are different, the Commission holds their education must be different. Men *are* different; but they are also the same. As the Commission points out, education in this country has failed in large part because it has emphasized those respects in which men are different; that is what excessive specialization means. The purpose of liberal or general education is to bring out our common humanity, a consummation more urgently needed today than at any time within the last five hundred years. To confuse at every point, as the Commission does, the education of our common humanity, which is primary and fundamental, with the education of our individual differences, which is secondary and in many cases unnecessary, is to get bad education at every point.

VIII

As we have seen, the Commission's principal reason for demanding greater diversification is that it proposes to double the number of students beyond the twelfth grade by 1960. The basis for this proposal is the revelation, provided by the Army General Classification Test, that at least 49 percent of the college-age population of the country has the ability to complete the first two years of college work, and at least 32 percent has the ability to complete additional years of higher education. ". . . these percentage figures supply conservative yet conclusive evidence of the social advisability of increased numbers attending college" (II, 7).

These percentage figures supply some evidence that a larger proportion of the college-age population has the ability to complete certain years of college. They supply no evidence whatever of the social advisability of having them do so. The argument that they should do so is based on the proposition that they have as much ability as those who are in college now. To know whether it is socially desirable to have them go to college, we should have to know whether it is socially desirable for all those who are in college now to be there, a question on which the Commission offers no evidence, and we should have to know why those who are not in college are not there. For example, it does not seem self-evident that a young man of twenty should be in the junior year in college if he prefers to be somewhere else.

Every citizen of a free society is entitled to a liberal education. This is the education which develops his intellectual power and the humanity which he has in common with his fellow-men. The first object of American educators should be to determine what a liberal education is; the second should be to discover the organization of the curriculum and of the educational system which will permit the student to acquire a liberal education in the shortest period of time. Father Gannon of Fordham has suggested that

through a six-year elementary school, a three-year high school, and a three-year college the student can get a liberal education by the time he is eighteen. There is plenty of evidence that the 6–4–4 plan permits the acquisition of liberal education by the age of nineteen or twenty.

This program requires the rigorous exclusion of triviality, frivolity, and duplication from the educational system. The student cannot get a liberal education by the age of eighteen or twenty if he has to be taught eleven basic outcomes; he cannot do it on the 8–4–2–2 plan. Nor can he do it if it is assumed that everything which might be useful or interesting to the citizen can and should be taught him in his youth. One of the reasons why the education of adults should be greatly expanded is that many things can be really learned only in adult life. Sir Richard Livingstone has taught us long since that for this reason the cultural level of a country cannot be automatically raised by the simple expedient of raising the school-leaving age.

Up to the point at which they have acquired a liberal education, then, we have an obligation to have all our youth, not 49 percent, but all, in college. Beyond that point education is a privilege, not a right. Its continuation beyond that point must chiefly depend on ability and interest. The Commission makes an appalling statement about interest: "Further, many individual young people offset their economic handicaps with cultural aspirations, ambition, and a driving thirst for knowledge that lead them to attempt to work their way through college if such a path is opened up to them. Yet such individual efforts will necessarily be the exception and are not palliatives to adverse conditions." (II, 11. Can the Commission mean that such efforts are mere palliatives?)

I am opposed to the prevailing superstition that it is a good thing for a boy to work his way through college; but the implication that cultural aspirations, ambition, and a driving thirst for knowledge are to be regarded as exceptional in our colleges has dreadful consequences; for these are precisely the qualifications for advanced study. Without them nobody should be admitted to it.

If everybody were in school or college until he had acquired a liberal education, and if beyond that only those were admitted who had the interest and ability that advanced study requires, we should have far more students up to the ages of eighteen or twenty and far fewer over those ages. The number of students we have should not be based on the number or on the ability of those we have now. It should be based on a clear definition of the purpose of each unit of the educational system.

IX

At the present time the omnibus is not going anywhere in particular, or rather, it is going off in all directions at once. The problem of higher education in America is not the problem of quantity. Whatever our shortcomings in this regard, we have a larger proportion of our young people in higher education than any country I can think of; and we certainly have more teachers and more square feet per student in bigger, newer buildings than any other nation in the world.

Neither the proportion of the population in school, nor the length of their schooling, nor the amount of money spent on it is an index to the educational requirements of a people, *unless* it is first established that the educational system under discussion is headed in the right direction. To increase the number of students, to prolong the period of their incarceration in schools, to spend twice the money, but spend it in the same way, when the system is headed in no direction, or in the wrong direction, or in all directions at once — these things will merely add to the embarrassments of the taxpayer; they will not promote the moral and intellectual development of our people.

What America needs, what the world needs, is a moral, intellectual, and spiritual revolution. Higher education in America fails unless it does what it can to initiate and carry through this revolution. This revolution will not be assisted by the infinite multiplication of trivial courses, of buildings, students, professors, salaries, or of colleges and universities. It will come only when the educators of America are willing to admit that the revolution must come and that they must make their contribution to it. It will come only when they are ready to forget their vested interests and try to see what the revolution will involve and how higher education should be related to it. The educators of America will be entitled to the support they demand when they can show that they know where they are going and why. The report of the President's Commission on Higher Education suggests that the time is still far off.

Byron S. Hollinshead: COLLEGES OF FREEDOM

IN last summer's issue of the *Bulletin* of the American Association of University Professors I tried to present an analysis of what seemed to me to be some of the chief faults of *The Report of the President's Commission*. In this paper I am more concerned to develop a platform to support an appeal to our fellow-Americans from the colleges and universities which are supported independently of the state. Such a platform needs contributions from many individuals, and it needs all the circulation we can give it if we are not to be swamped by the present and future deluge of taxpayers' money going to the support of public colleges.

My first contention is that freedom depends on the maintenance of a goodly number of independent institutions. I have heard one president and one vice president of Big Nine state universities say recently that the freedom of their institutions depended on the continuance of the University of Chicago and of Northwestern University. As Raymond Fosdick has said: "State colleges and universities have frequently been jeopardized by the arbitrary acts of those who hold political power. When that time comes the private institutions must be the counteracting agencies to keep the light of freedom burning. When Governor Talmadge terrorized the University of Georgia it was institutions like Emory University, Agnes Scott College and Mercer University that maintained in the state the basic decencies of independence. The steadying influence of Tulane University in the days of Huey Long in Louisiana cannot be overestimated. When the Board of Regents in Texas recently threatened the integrity of the state institutions, it was Rice Institute and Southern Methodist University that held the banner of free scholarship."

But I think there is a much more important reason than the foregoing for maintaining voluntary institutions. It lies in our whole heritage. The Pilgrims came to America because they wanted to worship God as they chose. Churches and other groups have established colleges to represent one view or another. It has always been very important for our way of life that these diverse views be represented. It has portrayed a willingness to let differing notions of truth be presented to compete with each other in the marketplace of ideas. It would be impossible to exaggerate the importance of allowing this diversity, for all our thought is molded and influenced by the varying influences of one doctrine in competition with another. This is possible only with a lot of separate institutions free to present different views of truth. You may think diversity would still prevail if all our higher institutions were public. Would it? In the public high schools some states are now going in for the state adoption of textbooks. Does this make for diversity? Is it impossible that the Association of Land-Grant Colleges, let us say, might sometime in the future decide on a uniform course of study with uniform materials? What would prevent it? And would the advance of truth be

Reprinted by permission from *Association of American Colleges Bulletin*, XXXV (1949), 62–73. Byron S. Hollinshead is President, Coe College.

served that way? Is there anyone in any statehouse or in Washington who should say what is the theory we should teach in astronomy, geology, economics or philosophy? If there is now a tendency for state adoption of textbooks and syllabi in secondary schools, what would prevent similar control of higher education if it came largely under public auspices?

My second point is that the independently-controlled colleges are less expensive to operate for the same reason that any independent agency can operate more efficiently and at lower expense than a similar agency of government. This is entirely aside from cost to the taxpayers. In Iowa, for next year, the public higher institutions are asking the Legislature for annual support of $25,000,000 to educate 23,000 students. (It will doubtless be argued that state colleges and universities maintain expensive graduate schools and provide services not related to teaching costs. This is certainly true. One of the institutions to which I am referring maintains a medical school which is, of course, very expensive. However, there are also other sources of income I have not mentioned. There are gifts and endowment income; there is Federal Smith-Hughes money, and there is income from the Veterans Administration. The last item was reported in the newspapers as $2,000,000 a year for one of the institutions. These extra sources of income should about balance costs beyond normal. It may also be that the comparison here made for Iowa is not altogether typical. Average annual costs per college student seem to be around $550.) They probably won't get this much but if they did this is an annual subsidy of over $1,000 per student plus tuition of $135 and up per student. The privately-controlled institutions could supply tuition, room and board for the same

figure. In fact, the State Board of Higher Education is asking for $25,000,000 per year for operation plus an asking of $32,000,000 for the biennium for capital improvements. Thus if we add $25,000,000 plus one half of $32,000,000 we get $41,000,000 as the proposed yearly appropriation for the next two years. There are somewhat less than 25,000 graduates of Iowa high schools yearly. Even if one half these went to college, it would be cheaper for the state to give the 12,500 who might conceivably attend college checks for $3,000 each on their graduation nights than it would be to maintain the state institutions. With the $3,000 the graduates could get room, board and tuition for three years at independently-controlled colleges. Last year the higher institutions of Iowa took an amount equivalent to the total collection of state income tax, levied at quite a high rate.

Some of my friends say: "Well, you don't want to join the Taxpayers' League, do you?" I'm not sure that I don't, because I see no stopping point. In Iowa we want to spend as much for higher education as Illinois which has three times the population. We want to spend as much at Ames as at Iowa City. Thus we see the curious spectacle of the taxpayer competing with himself and also competing with taxpayers of adjoining states in the race to make that president the hero who gets most from his legislature.

If it does seem desirable to educate everybody in whatever they can take and to keep half of them in school until they are twenty and one third of them until they are twenty-two as *The Report of the President's Commission* suggests, then the obvious way to do that economically is by establishing junior colleges in every city over 10,000 and diverting the money which is presently pouring into those state colleges which are poorly-located from them to local institutions. Even with the vast sums they are now receiving from legislatures, state colleges and universities are by no means inexpensive for students to attend.

But, in any case, taxes have now reached a point of great danger to our economy. In my relations with business and professional people I find entirely too many decisions about producing things or services are being made on the basis of how a given project, whatever it may be, will affect them taxwise. It is quite possible to develop an extensive black market to escape taxes and we are now close to that point.

My contention from the foregoing is that independent colleges not only can do the same or a better job more cheaply, but that voluntary support does not create the tax problems which may one day destroy our free system.

My third point is that if we are to preserve standards in education we must preserve independent colleges and universities. In support of this view all I need do is quote from the standards which *The Report of the President's Commission* proposes. It says that forty-nine per cent of the age group should be educated through the second year of college. Forty-nine per cent is more than the number now graduating from high school and such a proposal represents a belief that all those with I.Q. 100 or over can be successful college students. Actually, the standard would have to be lower than 100 I.Q. because, inevitably, there would be a large proportion who wouldn't go — girls who would get married, boys who would go into papa's business, youngsters who would go into the Armed Services, etc., and thus the standard would have to go down to I.Q. 95 or lower to get the number the Commission

proposes. Yet the studies of Thorndike indicate that it takes a fourteen-year old with an I.Q. of 110 to master algebra, and the experience of the high schools seems to bear this out.

Of course, no single indice is completely valid for making a decision about who should go to college. I should certainly not want to make a judgment based solely on the I.Q. Further, there are many types of abilities which an I.Q. test, or for that matter, the tests on which the Commission bases its judgment, does not measure. However, I think most psychologists would agree that I.Q. 110 is about as low as one can go if academic work is to deal with abstractions, rigorous analyses and is to assume any very exact or extensive vocabulary. According to Terman, less than twenty-five per cent of the population have I.Q.'s of 110 or above.

To be sure the Commission says there would need to be a great variety of courses appealing to a great variety of abilities. One can only exclaim, "how true." Yet such courses can hardly be defined as college work. The central purpose of a college, it seems to me, is the development of intellectual qualities which issue in responsible moral and spiritual outlooks. The courses the Commission proposes in general education to develop citizenship and a sense of heritage would be hard courses, harder perhaps than those we now give, if they are to accomplish what the Commission recommends.

The Commission makes an equally exciting assertion about how many should receive four years of college. Thirty-two per cent should go. This is two thirds of present high school graduates. The question is what subjects would they take in what college. According to Terman's distribution of intelligence again, this would mean that all those with I.Q. 105 or above should go through four years of college. Here again to get the number the Commission proposes we should need to go below those of I.Q. 105, say down to 100. Conceptual ability and abstract reasoning skill are very low with this group. Even the people who teach physical education classes would be stumped. In selecting the high school students who might be able successfully to pursue the technical courses of a regular four-year college program the Navy for the V–12 set an I.Q. of 117 as the minimum. The experience of the Navy and the experience of the colleges with this group, so far as I know, were eminently satisfactory. A lower minimum of around 115 I.Q., therefore, represents a good standard for a good college but only about twelve per cent of the population fall within the range of 115 I.Q. or over.

The Commission seems to reason something like this. Even if students have very low academic ability, they gain something by being in classes and by going to college. Is this so? Last year at the Iowa Philosophical Society meeting, a professor from a neighboring university was discussing a new course being offered in general education at that University called the History of Ideas. When he had concluded his description of the course one questioner asked: "I assume from what you say that there were three classifications of students in your course (which numbered 300 or so): A, those who followed your reasoning closely, saw nearly every point you made, and were stimulated by the course to go on with study of their own. Say these numbered about five per cent. B, those who gained a great deal from the course but whose main interests lay in other directions. Say these numbered about forty per cent. C, those without the wit to follow the lec-

ture or discussion, the patently bored who were only there by requirement. Say these numbered fifty-five per cent. Are these figures approximately correct, and, if so, what is the object in having the C group of fifty-five per cent there?"

The professor replied that he thought the classification into the three groups was correct, but that the percentages in groups A and B were overestimated. Probably the A group was closer to two per cent and the B group to ten per cent or fifteen per cent. He commented that the C group read newspapers, comic books, talked with seatmates or engaged in vacant stares while he lectured.

Now the point I want to make is that there is a serious and sincere difference of opinion about group C. The Commission apparently feels that it is an advantage for them to be in college, and it says that better teaching methods and less intellectuality in subject matter might reach them. I should be willing to grant that better teaching methods might reach a small percentage of them, but it seems to me that if we have the C group in our colleges in large numbers we inevitably pull down our standards and we do no favor to them. We take away from them valuable time during which they might be gaining an economic foothold. We give them no sense of mastery or self-confidence, and we engage them in an activity which, in my opinion, does not improve their vocational, individual or social competence. There is such a thing with a mechanical gadget perhaps as cheapening it but retaining some of its value. In much of education — understanding of an idea, a theorem, an hypothesis, a poem, a play — to cheapen is to destroy.

In this respect it seems to me that to increase public higher education and thereby to make dubious the existence of independent institutions is not only to lower general standards, but it is also to take away from the very gifted the opportunities they now have to develop themselves by especially rigorous training in competition with their peers. In this connection President Karl Compton has some important statements in the *President's Report for Massachusetts Institute of Technology for 1947*. Speaking of the increase in public higher education, President Compton says: "The most obvious danger is that the entire program of higher education will be brought to a mass level which at the worst could be mediocre and at the best could be rather far from optimum. . . . The political factors are against long-term emphasis on quality in state institutions because it is politically difficult to justify under governmental auspices a higher grade of opportunity for one person than for another. The political tendency is always toward equality of distribution."

My fourth contention is that democracy, as we know it, cannot survive unless its citizens possess a high degree of individual morality. It is also my belief, as Immanuel Kant has said, that morality depends to a very large degree on postulates of belief. Here I should like to make what seems to me to be a very important distinction which the *Report of the President's Commission* does not stress. That *Report* lumps colleges and universities into two general classifications, publicly-controlled and privately-controlled. The classification might well have gone further. There are publicly-controlled colleges and universities, there are colleges and universities not controlled either by the church or by the state, and there are denominational colleges and universities. The three types of control governing these institutions are quite different one from another.

The purely denominational colleges belong to their churches, the public colleges belong to the separate states, the colleges independent of church and state belong to their constituencies, and, in a broad sense, to the whole country. Now each of these types doubtless fosters morality to a degree. But it is my belief that the denominational and the independent colleges do it most successfully. Earlier I made the argument that the allowance of diversity of belief fosters truth. In much the same way allowance of denominationalism, which means differing theologies, not only is an aid toward arriving at truth but it also helps us to keep our society free by giving latitude to minorities with special contributions to make. Further, the differing theologies all seem to issue in the desirable fruit of morality. I may not be able to agree with my Catholic friends about their theology, but the fruit of morality which comes from Catholic theology seems to me to be wholly admirable. I may not agree with Methodist theology but I am for the morality it produces. I doubt if I could share the theological beliefs of Seventh Day Adventists, but I am sure their theology produces good morality.

Many denominational and some independent colleges have required courses in theology and ethics, have required chapel attendance, have ministers on their regular faculty and they can and do try to see that their theology, whatever it may be, issues in morality.

Those colleges independent both of church and state have moral purpose also. (I include with this group the church-related colleges.) Their conviction may be broader than a denominational belief and it is to be grasped only by some such phrase as "dedication to the liberal arts tradition" with its emphasis on goodness, beauty and truth. This purpose is just as real and just as vital as a sectarian theology which it may include since it possesses strong moral convictions and since it bases itself on the immortal teachings of the greatest poets, philosophers and men of God. It stems from Plato and Aristotle, from Christ and the Hebraic prophets, from Saint Paul and Saint Augustine, from Cicero and Dante, from Chaucer and Shakespeare, from Milton, Wordsworth, Newman, and Matthew Arnold, from Jefferson and Lincoln. It is a timeless creed of goodness, wisdom, justice and tolerance issuing in our concepts of the nature of man and of God, what the good society might be, and what the nature of our physical environment is.

It would certainly not be true to say that our public colleges do not possess also much of the value of this liberal tradition. They do. But by their very nature they are more susceptible to the pressures of immediacy. They are preoccupied with meeting needs, many of them vocational, and some of them important, which have little relation to the liberal tradition. The farmers can tell the land-grant colleges what they want; business men may object to time spent on the cultural heritage. Their students frequently go from two years of general education into more or less professional schools; whereas in the liberal arts colleges students are apt to be under liberal arts influence for four years. The public is far from wise about education and it makes immediate demands which may defeat altogether the broad purposes of philosophy.

Yet man cannot live by bread alone, nor can a free society survive without a spiritual outlook fostered either by denominationalism or by strong moral conviction and belief based on the liberal tradition. Therefore, it seems to me that if we are to have the moral purpose on which democracy depends we must preserve and foster both our denominational and independent colleges.

In summary, then, I have tried to present four plans in the platform we must write in developing the case of the college independent of the state. One, in the very nature of things, such colleges can with less difficulty than public institutions maintain academic standards. Two, they can do the educational job at less cost and without so much dependence on the taxpayer. Three, they alone can maintain the diversity which contributes to the freedom a democratic society must have if it is to progress toward truth; and, four, because they have spiritual purpose they can develop morality in students to a greater degree than an agency of the state can. . . .

Further, the independent and denominational colleges are desperately in need of help for equipment and capital improvements. They can expand if need be if they can get assistance on their building and equipment requirements. The government now has a matching funds program with the voluntary hospitals which serve all. I see no danger of federal control in such assistance and I hope the federal government will engage in similar arrangements with those independent colleges which serve all types of citizens.

I do not know how this should be arranged, but I should think a yearly contribution from the federal government of 3% (based on building depreciation costs of 1½ to 2 per cent and depreciation on equipment of 3 to 10 per cent) of the total value of buildings and equipment, or a yearly contribution based on average capital equipment costs per individual student would do it. Such a contribution would follow the practice of England

and the Dominions of yearly grants without strings attached to independent, non-profit, tax-exempt colleges and universities.

A generous program of student scholarships, then, for the half million students who need them, allowing such students to use their scholarships at denominational, independent or public colleges, and annual federal support without strings of a percentage of the value of buildings and equipment or based on capital costs per student to privately-controlled colleges would go a long way toward meeting the needs of which *The Report of the President's Commission* speaks. This assumes that local public junior colleges would be thought of as in California as a part of the public school system and that they would depend for support on the students, the local taxpayers, and the state.

The program here too briefly outlined would be far less expensive than the proposals of the President's Commission. I believe it would meet the broad social needs of our people and that it also would enable our country to keep alive those independent and denominational colleges which *The Report of the President's Commission* refers to as "safeguards of freedom."

NOTE: The Editor [of the *Association of American Colleges Bulletin*] is glad to print the following statements received from President Virgil M. Hancher of the State University of Iowa concerning that portion of point two referring to the state-supported institutions of higher learning in Iowa:

1. The statements in point two of President Hollinshead's address with reference to the Iowa State Board of Education and the institutions governed by it give the erroneous impression that the Board in its requests to the present Governor and General Assembly is asking $25,000,000 annually for the education of approximately 23,000 students.

2. President Hollinshead's statement concerning gifts, endowment income, federal Smith-Hughes money and income from the Veterans Administration does not correct this erroneous impression. With the exception of payments from the Veterans Administration, the items are either insignificant in amount or are devoted almost entirely to research and extension and not to the teaching of students. The payments from the Veterans Administration obviously refer to past transactions and, as everyone knows, will not continue into future years. In fact, their prospective decline is one of the bases for the Board's increased askings.

3. Of the Board's requests for $25,000,000 annually, not less than $9,000,000 were requested for public services (the Schools for the Blind, the Deaf, for Severely Handicapped Children, the Psychopathic Hospital, the State Sanatorium, the State Hygienic Laboratories and the University Hospital for the state indigent) no part of which could or should be charged to the cost of instruction in fields of higher learning. This is an obvious error of $9,000,000 out of a total of $25,000,000. Further cost accounting would increase, rather than diminish, this error.

4. President Hollinshead in his second point also says that the Board's askings amount to $1,000 of tax money for each student in each year of the biennium. He compares this sum unfavorably with the cost per student in liberal arts colleges. It is not clear what is being compared — whether the cost of liberal arts education is being compared with the cost of medical, dental and other professional education, or whether liberal arts education in the state institutions under the Iowa State Board of Education is being compared to liberal arts education in private colleges. The State University of Iowa is the only institution under the Board having a College of Liberal Arts. If the University were to receive the annual appropriations requested, the cost to the taxpayers of Iowa for the instruction of each undergraduate liberal arts student in the University would be less than $500 rather than $1,000 annually. This is an error of more than 100 per cent.

Allan P. Farrell: REPORT OF THE PRESIDENT'S COMMISSION: A CRITICAL APPRAISAL

ON two or three occasions when the report of the President's Commission on Higher Education was under discussion, one or other member of the Commission expressed surprise and a certain resentment at critical comments on the report, as if the criticism misrepresented the sentiments and beliefs of the Commission and questioned, if not its competence, at least its good faith. This attempt, therefore, at a critical appraisal of the report should begin with a disavowal and a declaration. Even the most outspoken critics of certain of the recommendations have not gone so far as to condemn the report as a whole; much less have they shown any inclination to indulge in a personal attack on the Commission itself or to hold individual members responsible for every detail of the report. The report is a public document of the greatest concern to the future of American higher education, and what it says, not what members of the Commission hold as private views or meant to say, must be the basis of debate and judgment.

All parties endorse the Commission's prime contention that neither the economic condition of a young person's parents nor his race, color, or creed should determine his educational opportunities. There is generous agreement, too, with several of the proposals for making educational opportunities available to more people, such as a national program of federally financed scholarships and fellowships, an expansion of community or junior colleges, and greatly increased opportunities and facilities open to adults. Similarly, the Commission's criticism of such things as excessive specialization in undergraduate colleges and the failure of graduate schools to train prospective college teachers in the art of teaching has been widely accepted as both right and sound.

Thereupon agreement ends and debate begins. And since it is important to keep the debate centered on major issues, we shall limit it here to the following six areas: (1) enrollment predictions, i.e., the number of qualified youth who might go to college if they had the money; (2) liberal vs. general education; (3) the status of nonpublic education; (4) the financial structure; (5) the participation of government; (6) the philosophy of the report.

Two Fundamental Weaknesses

The critical article which Chancellor Robert M. Hutchins wrote for the April 1948 *Educational Record*[1] points up two glaring weaknesses in the report that lessen confidence in its competence and prejudice judgment on the significant issues that the Commission raised and attempted to settle. These two weaknesses are: (1) the powerful support it gives to "the omnibus fallacy, the doctrine that education, more education,

[1] "The Report of the President's Commission on Higher Education," pp. 107–22.

Reprinted by permission from *Journal of Educational Sociology*, XXII, No. 8 (April, 1949), 508–522. Rev. Allan P. Farrell, of the University of Detroit, is Education Editor of *America*.

more expensive education, will solve every problem and answer every prayer," and (2) its tantalizing contradictions and qualifications that make it possible for anyone to prove almost anything from the report.

Father Gannon of Fordham called the omnibus fallacy by the name of educational inflation, i.e., proposing "a panacea for the intellectual and moral crisis through which the country is passing by offering more and more schooling, even if it be, as it will be, inferior."[2] President Wriston of Brown, if he is quoted correctly, made much the same point by comparing the report of the American Youth Commission published in the thirties with the 1948 report of the President's Commission: the former reflected the defeatist pessimism of the depression days as the latter reflects the optimism of an era of inflation. Dr. Hutchins quotes an example of what he calls the omnibus fallacy from Volume II, page 6, of the report:

This Commission . . . affirms the need of each individual for a broad educational experience. One which is not only general and liberal, not only sufficiently vocational, not only for broad competence in citizenship and in the wise use of leisure, but also an integrated and meaningful combination of all these aims at successive levels of education in accordance with the potentialities of each.

Another illustration, as well as a consequence, of the omnibus fallacy, are the contradictions and qualifications that make rational discussion of what the Commission actually said almost an impossibility. You are sure the Commission is for relaxed standards. But read what

[2] Address at the 94th annual dinner, Fordham Alumni Association, New York, February 9, 1948.

it says on page 44 of Volume I, that "the measure to which extended educational opportunities accomplish our purposes will depend on the kind of education provided." You quote from page 6 of Volume I to the effect that the Commission will not have "eternal" truths revealed in earlier ages applied to present and future problems, and on page 11 you find the Commission saying solemnly that "the everlasting moral essence of democracy lies in its fundamental principles, not in its means and methods of the moment." A revision by somebody who can substitute English for "pedagoguese" is needed.

Estimates of Enrollment

The Commission's prediction of a 4,600,000 enrollment in American colleges and universities by 1960 involves both a quantity and a quality estimate. Granted that 49 per cent of high-school graduates are capable of two more years of schooling and 32 per cent capable of a full college course, would that large a percentage *want* to go to college? That is the quantity issue. But *are* the 32 per cent really capable of a four year college education of good standard? That is the quality issue. Both of these issues have a close relationship to the Commission's planning and to its proposals.

The prediction that by 1960 as many as 49 per cent of our youth will want to go to college is believed to be optimistic. The reasons are two: first, because "only about forty-five per cent of the age group now graduate from high school," and second, because "even in states like California and Utah, where a high proportion now graduate from high school and have free junior colleges to attend, the proportion of those attending junior colleges is seldom over fifty per cent of the high-school graduates. This means that the total attendance, even for two years, in places where the situation has been optimum has not been over one-third of the age group."[3]

One factor militating against the Commission's estimate is that of motivation. Robert J. Havighurst and his associates, who have made studies of lower-middle and lower-class families in several midwestern communities, found that "fully as many able young people fail to go to college because they lack the desire as those who fail to go because they lack the money."[4] Their conclusion in regard to the Commission's estimate is this: "Making the most optimistic assumptions — that half of all lower-middle and lower-class youth have sufficient intellectual ability to go to college and that half of this group who are not now in college would go if they had financial assistance . . . an additional 18 per cent would attend college . . . making a total of 35 per cent. This is to be compared with the Commission's recommendation of 50 per cent."[5] Thus Byron S. Hollinshead, following Havighurst's calculations, says: "We might have a college enrollment by 1960 of 3,000,000 students, or double the pre-World War II enrollment, but certainly not the triple figure of 4,600,000 estimated by the Commission. The figure I have just given agrees with an independent estimate made by Dr. Harry K.

Newburn, President of the University of Oregon."[6]

Disagreement over the percentage of youth who are capable of two more years of schooling and the percentage capable of a full college course is basically a question of whether the Commission had good grounds for its estimate that all students who rank in the seventh percentile of the American Council on Education Psychological Examination have a "reasonable expectation" of completing the 14th school year and those who rank in the twenty-first percentile a "reasonable expectation" of completing college. President Seymour of Yale believes that if we accept the proposed expansion program before we improve the quality of the education we give, we will endanger the quality of the whole educational fabric.[7]

Force is given to these views that an increase in numbers will lower the quality of higher education by the Commission's own description of the kind of education it wants in the colleges of the future — an education that will "provide programs for the development of other abilities than those involved in academic aptitude" (I, 32), an education that will build programs of concentration in the senior college "around a much wider range of intellectual and occupational objectives to serve a much larger and less selected body of students" (I, 72), an education that will put less emphasis on "the present orientation of higher education toward verbal skills and intellectual interests" (I, 32).

In one of its main sections on the community college (I, 68), the Commission appears to agree that the quality of edu-

[3] Byron S. Hollinshead, "The Report of the President's Commission on Higher Education," *Bulletin* of the Association of American University Professors, XXXIV, No. 2 (summer 1948), 260–61.

[4] Robert J. Havighurst, "Social Implications of the Report of the President's Commission on Higher Education," *School and Society*, April 3, 1948, p. 259.

[5] *Ibid.*, p. 260.

[6] *Op. cit.*, p. 258.

[7] Reported in *The New York Times* of February 24, 1948.

cation at the community-college level would be different, and lower, than in a four year liberal-arts college, and it adds significantly (I, 70) that "in many cases these students will be stimulated to continue their college careers *if the 4-year colleges will meet them halfway with liberal admission policies*" (italics added). The catch is that if the community-college standard would be as different as indicated, the admission policies of four year liberal-arts colleges would have to be too liberal on the side of quality for their own good. It may be that this fact has some connection with the Commission's attitude on general vs. liberal education.

General vs. Liberal Education

Chancellor Hutchins has remarked that "the Commission never misses a chance to communicate the news that our educational institutions are too intellectual."[8] And he goes on to illustrate:

The Commission deplores "the present orientation of higher education towards verbal skills and intellectual interests" (I, 32). It says that American schools and colleges are preoccupied with the training of the intellect. It even thinks that faculty meetings are too intellectual and recommends "deliberations which have some immediate results, such as the purchase of new movie projectors, or the issuance of a career guidebook for students" (IV, 40). It urges administrators to be irrational. "Administrators tend to think in terms of a logical approach to curriculum problems — formulating an over-all philosophy first, then stating broad objectives, appraising the present program in terms of those objectives, defining weaknesses, and discovering ways to eliminate them. Experience demonstrates that this approach is likely to be unproductive of the one essential change, a change in the thinking and teaching and research activities of individual faculty members" (IV, 41).

And so we end up with a college in which neither the students, the faculty, nor the officers are supposed to think, or, at least, to look as though they were thinking.[9]

Despite its seeming exaggeration, this blunt critique could be further documented from Volumes I and II of the report (e.g., I, 32, 44, 58, 59; II, 7, 41, 42).

The question to be answered is: How, in the Commission's mind, does "general" differ from liberal education? "General education should give to the student the values, attitudes, knowledge, and skills that will equip him to live rightly and well in a free society. It should enable him to identify, interpret, select and build into his own life those components of his cultural heritage that contribute richly to understanding and appreciation of the world in which he lives. It should therefore embrace ethical values, scientific generalizations, and aesthetic conceptions, as well as an understanding of the purposes and character of the political, economic and social institutions that men have devised" (I, 49). "Thus conceived," the Commission continues, "general education is not sharply distinguished from liberal education; the two differ mainly in degree, not in kind. General education undertakes to redefine liberal education in terms of life's problems as men face them, to give it human orientation and social direction, to invest it with content that is directly relevant to the demands of contemporary society. General education is liberal education with its matter and method shifted from its original aristocratic intent to the service of democracy" (I, 49).

After debating these concepts and distinctions, the Commission on Liberal Education of the Association of American Colleges came to the conclusion that

8 *Op. cit.*, p. 117.

9 *Ibid.*

they "not only betray a basic confusion upon what constitutes general and what liberal education, but will be misinterpreted as an attack upon liberal education as such."[10] Perhaps the fundamental difference in the Commission's concept of liberal education lies in the different emphasis put on the social and individual role of education. In the Commission's report (I, 5, 6, 47) the social role is given primacy, and nowhere does the individual and human character of traditional liberal education gain the attention it deserves. There is the statement that "the first goal in education for democracy is the full, rounded and continuing development of the person" (I, 9). But like so many other statements in the report, this is so often contradicted or qualified as to lead one to the conviction that to the Commission's way of thinking the "development of the person" is not a good in itself, but only good in so far as it serves the ends of democracy. At any rate, the report puts much more emphasis on social than on intellectual development and views education dominantly in terms of democracy rather than in terms of the individual.

In his paper, "The President Studies Higher Education,"[11] Gould Wickey notes this overemphasis on the social as compared with the personal or individual in education. "It is true," he says, "President Truman in his letter of appointment of Commission members called attention to the necessity of reexamining 'our system of higher education in terms of its objectives, methods, and facilities; and *in light of the social role it has to play.*' That last clause seems to mislead the Commission for their report might just as well

have been entitled, 'Education for Citizenship.' " Certainly no one should underestimate the social role of education. But man is not for society any more than he is for the state. The philosophy of the report, which will be gone into later, lays down a purely naturalistic philosophy of man, society, and the state. Instead of viewing democracy as a fair field for cultivating the good life, it turns democracy into the Good Life, making of it a sort of religion, an end; and man, the student, seems to be projected as a means, an instrument to serve this end. That the true nature of man, as always understood in traditional liberal education, is nowhere acknowledged as of prime importance in "general" education, is enough to suggest that liberal and "general" education differ in kind as well as in degree.

Private Colleges, Finance, Government

The next three areas of debate — the Commission's attitude toward the privately controlled institutions, its pattern of finance, and the role of the state — are sufficiently interrelated to be dealt with as a unit. No other part of the report has aroused quite as much amazement, quite as much official flutter in academic dovecots, as what the Commission told the privately controlled colleges and universities. Somebody dubbed it a whispered "Hail" and a shouted "Farewell." "You have done as good a job as could be expected," it whispered. "Let us even call it a good job, a pioneer job. But of course it wasn't a big enough job. NOW we will take over," it boomed, "and our great state universities will do the big job, bigger and therefore better; costlier and bigger and therefore better. We hope you'll be able, somehow, to keep going."

Almost everybody agrees that this is pretty much the tone of Volume V of the report. It is said that Dr. George F. Zook,

---

[10] "Report of the Commission on Liberal Education," *Bulletin* of the Association of American Colleges, March 1948, p. 145.

[11] *Christian Education*, XXXI (June 1948), 100.

president of the American Council of Education, who acted as chairman of the President's Commission, has acknowledged as much and deprecated it.

One of the contributors to *Whither American Education?* suspects "a causal relationship between the Commission's small esteem of liberal education and its snubbing of privately-controlled institutions; for it is in the latter that the tradition of liberal education has been kept alive."[12] Perhaps there are better grounds for seeing a causal relationship rather between the report's social philosophy and its attitude toward the private colleges and universities. The viewpoint of that philosophy is that youth should be trained for the democratic state and that the democratic state is a sort of religion, with public education as its church. It would seem that to this social philosophy is due much of the Commission's strong preference for public education. The assumption is that "American democracy will be best served by a mighty system of public higher education to be financed by local, State, and Federal taxes, and to be controlled, managed, and supervised by governmental agencies."[13]

This means, frankly, that the thinking in the report is toward statism. A writer in the Catholic University of America *Bulletin* quotes two passages from Alexander Meiklejohn's *Education Between Two Worlds* (1942) to illustrate his thinking. "It is the State which is replacing the Church. It is government, national, provincial, and local, which has control of teaching. Education is not only becoming secular. It is also becoming political" (p. 3). And again: "For better or worse, we have chosen to put the girding, and

nurturing, and cultivating of the growth of our people into the hands of the State" (p. 8). To which the writer appends the comment: "From beginning to end, the President's Commission confirms Meiklejohn's statements. These eminent educators are apparently quite willing to turn over higher education in this country to the State, to make education political. The evidence is quite clear."[14]

Two members of the Commission, Mgr. Frederick G. Hochwalt and Dr. Martin R. P. McGuire, firmly dissented from the thinking of the majority of the Commission. Their dissent, printed at the end of Volume V of the report, issues this warning: "We fear that legislation implementing the Commission's recommendation would go a long way toward establishing an administrative structure for higher education whereby Government in the United States might easily use the nation's public colleges and universities to promote its political purposes" (V, 66). In subscribing "wholeheartedly" to this dissenting view, President Hollinshead of Coe College took occasion to quote what Raymond B. Fosdick wrote on "The Role of the Private College." "State colleges and universities," he said, "have frequently been jeopardized by the arbitrary acts of those who hold political power. When that time comes the private institutions must be the counteracting agencies to keep the light of freedom burning."[15]

The Commission itself said the same thing in the course of arguing against granting public funds in support of privately controlled colleges and universities. "The acceptance of public funds by

12 New York: America Press, p. 14.

13 *Higher Education for American Democracy*, Report of the President's Commission on Higher Education, "Statement of Dissent," V, 66.

14 Rev. Michael J. McKeough, Ord. Praem., "The President's Commission on Higher Education," Catholic University of America *Bulletin*, XVI (January 1949), 7.

15 Hollinshead, *op. cit.*, p. 264.

any institution, public or private, should carry with it the acceptance of the right of the people as a whole to exercise review and control of the educational policies and procedures of that institution. Such acceptance by privately controlled institutions would, in the opinion of this Commission, tend to destroy the competitive advantages and free inquiry which they have established and which are so important in providing certain safeguards to freedom. It would be contrary to the best interests of these institutions as well as to those of society in general" (V, 58). That the Commission was conscious of the great and real danger to privately controlled institutions in the extreme imbalance between public and private higher education as expressly envisioned in its recommendations, is evident from the statement it made elsewhere: "The Commission is . . . aware of the fact that its proposals for a great expansion of higher education in publicly controlled institutions may make it extremely difficult for many private institutions to survive" (V, 46).

What the Commission did not see or see clearly enough is well expressed by Gould Wickey when he said that "the basic philosophy of the report will tend to the development of an educational program in which the state and federal control over all higher education will be so tremendous that privately-supported schools will be affected whether aided or not. In not desiring to aid through federal funds the development of any religion or denomination in its educational institutions, the Commission has gone to the other extreme of devising a procedure which will result in a totalitarianism destructive of the very democracy in which they seem to be interested."[16] This is a

hard saying, but it was uttered by the two dissenting members of the Commission in a debate over the recommendations included in Volume V of the report, and fell on deaf ears.[17]

And so the very real dangers inherent in the Commission's attitude toward privately controlled colleges and universities (and toward private accrediting agencies as well) must be brought to the attention of the American public. It is no longer safe or sane to think that totalitarianism cannot happen here. This is not to say that the Commission believes in or wants totalitarianism to happen here. No doubt it would fiercely repudiate the very idea. What must be said is that the recommendations of the Commission, if accepted and implemented, would lead to statism, which is a form of totalitarianism.

Philosophy of the Report

To those who have criticized the philosophy of the report as reflecting naturalism or secularism, members of the Commission have pointed to page fifty of Volume I as sufficient refutation of the criticism. On that page there is a feeble statement to this effect: "Religion is held to be a major force in creating the system of human values on which democracy is predicated, and many derive from one or another of its varieties a deepened sense of human worth and a strengthened concern for the rights of others" (I, 50). On the same page the Commission refers to "spiritual and ethical development," "ethical considerations," and "faith in each other"; but it hurriedly adds: "Ethical principles that will induce this faith need not be based on any single sanction or be authoritarian in origin, nor need finality be claimed for them." Upon which Dr. Gould Wickey remarks: "In other

[16] *Op. cit.*, pp. 101–2.

[17] Cf., "Statement of Dissent," *op. cit.*, V, 66.

words, for the Commission moral principles are utilitarian and relative. And that
is just the reason education does not
know where it is going. It is based on
principles relative to the times rather
than on principles basic for all times. . . .
As for religion, the Commission admits
that religion *is held to be* a major force
in creating the system of human values
on which democracy is predicated. Since
some persons find a satisfactory basis for
a moral code in the democratic creed itself, some in philosophy, some in religion,
it is clear that religion is not absolutely
essential for human welfare, for the education of the free man, and for American
democracy."[18]

One of the members of the Commission sums up the philosophy of the report
in these words:

The motives and ends of action, the standards of judgment, the measure of accomplish-
ment, are all evaluated in terms of current
needs of American democratic society and
the democratic State. The ultimate end of
this society is its own greatest possible progress in all those aspects which it may consider
beneficial to itself at successive stages of development. In other words, this democratic
society is a materialistic society in process of
evolution. The democratic society of the Report is identical in name only with democratic society in the traditional and Christian
sense.

A superficial reading of the Commission's
Report, therefore, may give the impression
that the dominant philosophical outlook is
secularistic; but in reality it is much more
significant and positive than that. In the

Report, democracy is defined in terms of a
religion, and democracy is, in fact, very
definitely the religion of an ever increasing
number of Americans. Democracy is defined
as religious ideals are defined, and it is set
up as the ultimate inspiration and sanction
of action. The church of this democracy is
the public school.[19]

Should any one of several of the Commission's recommendations that have
been criticized in this perhaps annoy-
ingly critical paper be put into effect, the
eventual result would be to make the
youth of the nation wards of the state
from kindergarten through graduate and
professional school; and that would soon
produce the phenomenon of the dis-
appearance of young people as humanism and religion conceive them.

The report is bound to play an influ-
ential role in steering higher educational
policy in the United States for years to
come. In spite of the criticisms of its
fundamental philosophy and of a number of its recommendations, which have
been brought out in this "critical appraisal," it contains a wealth of solidly
established information, as well as many
suggestions and proposals that would
make for the improvement of all our colleges and universities. The report should
be studied critically but constructively.
Wide discussion of it will contribute to
whatever revisions and modifications may
be necessary in order to bring it into
harmony with our long-standing ideals
of democracy.

18 *Op. cit.*, pp. 97–98.

19 M. R. P. McGuire, "Blueprint for the New
American Education," *America*, April 3, 1948,
Sec. II, pp. 1–4.

T. R. McConnell: A REPLY TO THE CRITICS

THE debate stimulated by the report of the President's Commission on Higher Education has served to place squarely before the people some fundamental problems and issues in the future development of higher education in the United States. While some of the criticisms of the report seem to the present writer to be based on misinterpretations of its content, most of the opposition represents basic disagreement on matters of educational policy and program. The Commission was not unaware that these differences existed; criticism or opposition was therefore obviously not unexpected. The Commission simply chose to state what it considered its own best judgment with respect to the basic questions and issues which it discussed.

Many critics have strongly disagreed with the Commission's proposal for a great expansion of college enrollment. The Commission did not predict an enrollment of 4,600,000 beyond the twelfth grade by 1960. Rather, it presented this number of students as a desirable goal. There are reasons to believe, on purely practical grounds, that this goal is unlikely to be attained. Havighurst,[1] for example, has estimated that the motivational barrier is at least as important as the economic barrier in keeping young people out of college, and that removal of financial difficulties would raise the

proportion of young people who attend college to about 35 per cent, compared with the Commission's assumption of 50 per cent. The criticism that the Commission's goal is *unrealistic* is less significant for present consideration, however, than the contention that its objective is *undesirable*. It is possible to predict that college enrollment will reach only about 3,000,000 by 1960, without rejecting the Commission's belief that a much larger enrollment would be fully consistent with the whole of our educational, social, economic, political, and cultural development.

One critic, fearful that the colleges are threatened with "a tide of mediocrity," has condemned the Commission's proposal for expansion of enrollment in this somewhat immoderate language: "The fraud in the present campaign for educational inflation consists in spreading our national culture perilously thin and calling it 'democracy in education.' It consists in swelling the number of incompetents in American colleges and calling it 'equality of opportunity.' "[2] To this, President Jones of the University of Arkansas made the following reply: "I don't think much of that metaphor. It implies that culture is a substance like peanut butter, that we haven't much of it, and that if we try to share it more widely all the children will be skimped on their sandwiches. But knowledge, unlike pea-

[1] R. J. Havighurst, "Social Implications of the Report of the President's Commission on Higher Education," *School and Society*, LXVII (April 3, 1948), 257–61.

[2] R. I. Gannon, as reported in *The New York Times* of February 10, 1948.

Reprinted by permission from *Journal of Educational Sociology*, XXII, No. 8 (April, 1949), 533–551. T. R. McConnell is Chancellor, University of Buffalo. He was a member of the President's Commission.

nut butter, does *not* diminish by being shared. It is more likely to increase."[3]

President Seymour of Yale has deplored "the Commission's assumption that every boy and girl in America has 'a right' to go to college," and insisted that "a college education is a privilege, not a right."[4] The first part of this statement is, of course, inaccurate, and rather grossly so. The Commission took the position that approximately half, not all, young people have the intellectual capacity to complete at least fourteen years of schooling. The assertion that a college education is a "privilege" and not a "right" is a remnant of an aristocratic attitude that is of doubtful value in the present age. Although admitting that many Americans naively believe that will power and schooling can compensate for lack of general capacity and specific aptitudes, President Conant considers that "such leveling doctrines were the antibodies supplied unconsciously by the body politic to counteract the claims of those who had enjoyed 'the privileges of a higher education.' "[5] A democratic view of society and education does not hold that all individuals deserve, or can profit from, the same kind of education. The democratic ideal does imply, as President Jones has said, "the *right* of every individual to develop whatever excellence is in him."[6]

The short-sightedness of confining higher education to a select group I have emphasized in another place, as follows:

All education in the United States, elementary, secondary, and higher, is based on the belief that a democracy cannot exist and grow merely through the leadership of an intellectual elite. The recent development of both secondary and higher education in our country is an expression of the conviction that a modern democratic society must have a large body of citizens who possess a deep understanding of the problems of modern life; who are devoted to the purposes and ideals of a free society and who will take a responsible and enlightened part in public affairs, both national and international. Furthermore, there is a widespread feeling that the highly educated few are unlikely to be recognized or accepted as leaders in a democracy if the great body of citizens have no basis of communication with them. The problems of human society are not likely to be solved as long as there exists a great intellectual gulf between the highly educated few and the meagerly educated masses. The differences among citizens in a democracy should take the form of gradations instead of sharp distinctions between the uninformed and the enlightened, the uncultured and the cultivated, the vocationally and the liberally educated man.[7]

The report has been interpreted as opposing any form of selection of students by individual institutions. I can find nothing in the document which makes any such implication. The attitude of the report is more accurately characterized by the comment made recently by Dean Alva R. Davis of the University of California at Berkeley to the effect that "we all too frequently say that there are too many students in the university. This may be true, but we can't rid ourselves of responsibility by raising entrance

[3] L. W. Jones, "The Challenge of the President's Commission," mimeographed copy of an address delivered at the Sixty-second Annual Convention of the Association of Land-Grant Colleges and Universities, Washington, D. C., November 9, 1948.

[4] C. Seymour, as reported in *The New York Times* of March 14, 1948.

[5] J. B. Conant, *Education in a Divided World* (Cambridge: Harvard University Press, 1948), p. 208.

[6] *Op. cit.*

[7] T. R. McConnell, *Report of Preparatory Conference of Representatives of Universities* (Paris: United Nations Educational, Scientific, and Cultural Organization, 1948), pp. 145–46.

standards and then making faces over the scholastic fence at those excluded."[8] Neither by direct statement nor by implication does the report oppose the right of a private college or university, or for that matter of a public one, to select the students who are most likely to profit from its educational program. What the report does recommend is *a varied but comprehensive* pattern of institutions and curriculums that will meet the needs of many high-school graduates for education of different kinds and different extents. It did not propose that all students should take the same curriculum, that they could profit from the same length of training, or that they should be educated in the same sort of college or university. It envisaged an over-all program of rich diversity — community colleges, four year liberal-arts colleges, universities of complex organization combining general education and occupational training, professional colleges, and other specialized schools providing the diverse training that a highly complex society must have. The Commission's general blueprint for such a comprehensive system of post high-school education was neither visionary nor particularly novel. The *Report of the Temporary Commission on the Need for a State University* in New York outlined a state-wide plan on essentially the same broad lines, and the recent *Report on the Needs of California in Higher Education* presented a concrete example of the kind of over-all educational program the Commission had in mind, although it was developed quite independently of the Commission's deliberations.

8 A. R. Davis, "The Place of the Community College in a State Educational System," mimeographed copy of an address delivered at the Sixty-second Annual Convention of the Association of Land-Grant Colleges and Universities, Washington, D. C., November 10, 1948.

In a critique of the report of the President's Commission published under the auspices of the National Catholic Education Association in a pamphlet entitled, *Whither American Education?*, this passage appears: "Had the Commission said: we think that 49 per cent of our youth can take advantage of some sort of post-secondary education; many of these (with economic barriers removed) will be as able as any others to pass the admission standards and fulfill the graduation requirements of any college or university in the country; many others will need a different type of education, say, in terminal community colleges, which will capitalize on and develop capacities such as social sensitivity, motor skill, mechanical aptitude and ability to grasp abstractions —had the Commission said this, and suggested suitable programs for the new type of education, it would have performed a larger service to democracy."[9]

This is an amazing passage, because that is essentially what the Commission *did* say, with the important addition that with the fulfillment of particular aptitudes of whatever sort should go the fullest possible measure of general education for rich personal life and responsible citizenship.

One suspects that in certain instances the objection to expansion of educational opportunity as a threat to "standards" screens an aristocratic attitude toward higher education. But in other cases, I am sure, it represents a sincere fear that educational quality may be sacrificed and the gifted student neglected. It is not undemocratic to recognize and nurture exceptional talent. Our society needs all the talent it can find. But I do not believe that quantity and quality are incompatible, if society gives adequate support

9 Pp. 19–20.

to education. I agree with President Conant that "we must see to it that public support of education beyond the high school is consistent with our democratic ideals; without diminishing our concern for education for *all* American youth, we must seek more effective ways of finding and educating talent for the service of the nation."[10]

To this end, the Commission gave highest priority to its recommendation for a system of federal scholarships and fellowships granted on a competitive basis and usable in both private and public institutions. Perhaps, as President Conant has suggested, the full program proposed by the Commission is a bit too ambitious for the immediate future, but I do not agree with him that in the beginning the scholarships and fellowships should be limited to students headed for the professions of medicine, dentistry, public health, and for research careers in the natural sciences. The need for research in human relations is desperate, and I believe that the Congress can be persuaded to include the social sciences, humanities, and education with the physical and biological sciences in a comprehensive program.

On philosophical grounds, the report has been subjected to two broad criticisms: first, that it emphasized social to the neglect of individual values, and second, that it expressed a purely secular view of education.

The first criticism takes a variety of forms. One of the variants is that the Commission proceeded on the mistaken assumption that the purpose of education is to create a better society, whereas it is really to transform the individual. This doctrine is especially comforting to college and university presidents who must

solicit gifts from donors who do not approve free investigation of controversial political, economic, and social problems. President Wriston has asserted that the Commission's concern for human dignity and individual opportunity and freedom is inconsistent with its desire for more effective social technology. He has gone much further: he has charged that the concept of social engineering is "deeply authoritarian," since this concept, he declares, "deals with individuals not as persons of great value and dignity but as social units, a very different matter indeed."[11]

What did the Commission actually say about the relationship of the individual and society? Did it propose some new, or old, brand of totalitarianism? As requested by President Truman in his letter creating the Commission, it did "reexamine our system of higher education . . . in the light of the social role it has to play." Not by implication, but by explicit declaration early in the first volume of its report, the Commission recognized that the attainment of democratic values depends upon individual development. The following paragraphs from the report are in point:

The first goal in education for democracy is the full, rounded, and continuing development of the person. The discovery, training, and utilization of individual talents is of fundamental importance in a free society. To liberate and perfect the intrinsic powers of every citizen is the central purpose of democracy, and its furtherance of individual self-realization is its greatest glory.

A free society is necessarily composed of free citizens, and men are not made free solely by the absence of external restraints. Freedom is a function of the mind and the

[10] *Op. cit.*, p. 210.

[11] H. M. Wriston, from typed copy of an address on "Implications of the Report of the President's Commission on Higher Education."

spirit. It flows from strength of character, firmness of conviction, integrity of purpose. It is channeled by knowledge, understanding, and the exercise of discriminating judgment. It consists of freedom of thought and conscience in action. . . .

If our colleges and universities are to graduate individuals who have learned how to be free, they will have to concern themselves with the development of self-discipline and self-reliance, of ethical principles as a guide to conduct, of sensitivity to injustice and inequality, of insight into human motives and aspirations, of discriminating appreciation of a wide range of human values, of the spirit of democratic compromise and cooperation.[12]

This personal integrity and human sensitiveness seemed to the Commission to be a means of coupling individual development and freedom with social responsiveness and social responsibility. Is the idea that, working together freely and voluntarily, men might devise better social means of promoting human values a "deeply authoritarian" concept? For that is essentially what the Commission meant by its desire to see an improved social technology. It said: "It is essential that we apply our trained intelligence and creative imagination, our scientific methods of investigation, our skill in invention and adaptation, as fully to the problems of human association as to the extension of knowledge about the physical world. This is what is meant by the development of *social invention* and *social technology*."[13]

True, this process is not likely to maintain everything just as it is. "It should be expected," wrote President Turck, "that the more conservative groups in America will be disturbed by these declarations as to the use of social science and social technology. But should the heads of church-related colleges be disturbed? Only to the extent that such colleges represent a naive devotion to laissez faire in economics, 'that government is best which governs least' in political science, and the ancient law of tooth and nail, every man for himself and the Devil take the hindmost, in sociology. Unless we are prepared to abandon the social sciences, we must accept the challenge to use them for the common good. . . ."[14]

Another variant of the criticism of the report's emphasis on the social role of education is President Havens' fear that by accepting responsibility for inspiring students with enthusiasm for the democratic way of life, higher education may ultimately find "that it has been discredited by its alliance with an outworn philosophy of government" (see p. 524). Although I can speak only for myself, I should doubt that many members of the Commission would expect the fundamental conception of democracy to be so vulnerable to the test of time. If President Havens thinks the Commission meant that higher institutions should try to convince students that the political, social, and economic arrangements of the moment are perfect and final, the following statements in the report should allay his fears:

The processes and institutions of democracy are not static or fixed; it is essential that they be flexible, capable of adaptation to the changing needs and conditions of men. The everlasting moral essence of democracy lies in its fundamental principles, not in its means and methods of the moment.

. . . It is the responsibility of higher education to devise programs and methods which will make clear the ethical values and the

12 *Higher Education for American Democracy,* "Establishing the Goals," I, 9–10.
13 *Ibid.*, p. 20.

14 C. J. Turck, "The Immediate Goals of Higher Education in America," *College and Church,* XIII, No. 1 (1948), 13–16.

concept of human relations upon which our political system rests. Otherwise we are likely to cling to the letter of democracy and lose its spirit, to hold fast to its procedures when they no longer serve its ends, to propose and follow undemocratic courses of action in the very name of democracy.[15]

This framework would seem to give ample opportunity for the free exercise of intelligence, for a devoted search for the truth.

The criticism that the Commission gave too little recognition to the importance of religion in education also takes several forms. Many critics have taken the general position that the Commission's treatment of the place of religion in society and in education was basically inadequate. In some instances, however, the criticisms go beyond this general censure to object to certain statements on somewhat narrower theological or philosophical grounds. Their target is the statement, which follows several paragraphs on the importance of ideals, values, and ethical principles as educational outcomes, that "ethical principles . . . *need not* [italics mine] be based on any single sanction or be authoritative in origin, nor need finality be claimed for them."

Critics of this statement should recognize that not all religions treat the problem of authoritarianism in the same way, and that some religious groups might object as strongly to an authoritarian position as another might insist upon it. And perhaps the critics should note that the statement reads that "ethical principles . . . *need not* be based on any single sanction or be authoritarian in origin. . . ." The report does not condemn any individual or group which chooses to accept religious absolutism. It simply recognizes

that such a position as the following may also be taken by those who are interested in religion and in church-related colleges:

The church-related colleges of America in the twentieth century must not be led down the path of authoritarianism as opposed to freedom, nor up to the heights of revelation as opposed to scientific knowledge. These colleges have a less exalted destiny. They are institutions of learning and of teaching. They must not separate themselves from the great goals of the society of which they are a part.[16]

And a philosopher, President Taylor of Sarah Lawrence College, finds the doctrine of absolute and final values unacceptable, for in his review of the Commission's report, he wrote that education ". . . must deal with personal, spiritual, and social questions which concern life in the present and in the future. Some of these are the eternal questions of human destiny, freedom and the nature of life. They are eternal because they have appeared at each stage of the recurring present during the past centuries of Eastern and Western civilization. They have been answered in a variety of ways, by religious thinkers, poets, scientists, philosophers, novelists, and workers. . . . Since no one of the answers is absolute and complete, it is the responsibility of the scholar and of the student constantly to raise the great questions in the urgency of their present social and personal setting, and by the study and valuing of ideals and realities, by the careful and attentive consideration of the answers others in the past and present time have given, to make our own knowledge and values as best we can."[17]

16 C. J. Turck, *op. cit.*

17 H. Taylor, "On the Report of the President's Commission: The Future of American Education," *American Scholar*, XVIII, No. 1 (1948–49), 39–40.

15 *Op. cit.*, pp. 11–12.

In its treatment of general education, the Commission urged a program which, in President Conant's words, "should have relevance to the immediate future of our civilization,"[18] or which, as Sydney Hook expressed it, would put "central emphasis on the focal problems of our culture, and the intellectual skills and moral habits with which to cope with them."[19] To avoid any misunderstanding, the report explicitly disclaimed any adherence to the "cult of immediacy." It did not ask the college to neglect the past; it only followed Sydney Hook in insisting that education should not get lost in the past. The report underlined the importance of bringing the wisdom of the past to bear on the present, not for the purpose of reproducing an old world but of making a better, a more human and humane one. The attitude with which this kind of general education approaches the past is, in the words of Professor J. W. Beach of the University of Minnesota, "not merely of interpreting the present in the light of the great tradition, but also of interpreting and appraising the great tradition in the light of present ideas, present problems, and present knowledge."[20]

It has been said that general education characterized by this spirit and purpose "differs not merely in degree but in kind from genuine liberal education," and that it is essentially "anti-intellectual."[21] Is an education that emphasizes the application of intellect to the affairs of men illiberal or anti-intellectual? If so, Milton must have been confused

when he defined "a compleat and generous Education" as that "which fits a man to perform justly, skilfully and magnanimously all the offices both private and public of Peace and War."

Some critics seem to take the position that the Commission *should* have made a distinction in kind between general and liberal education. But, I take it, the Commission quite deliberately stressed the harmony between general education and a truly liberal education, i.e., an education which, according to President Conant's analysis, is devoted to education for the good life and for intelligent and active citizenship.[22] In suggesting that the only important difference between "general" and "liberal" education might be one of degree rather than kind, the Commission had in mind, I take it, the importance of extending to all students, whatever their fields of specialization, at least a minimum experience with liberal studies. If the student's intellectual capacity, the demands of his professional education, and his financial resources make it possible for him to take the time for a fuller and deeper liberal education — either before or along with his specialized work — so much the better. But differences in degree need not nullify the underlying unity of spirit which it is the purpose of general education to inspire.

The Commission has been accused of being disinterested in private higher education, and in some instances of being actually hostile to it. It is difficult to understand how the Commission could have been either. A glance at its membership will reveal that a majority of the academic members and laymen taken together were directly connected with private colleges or private universities,

18 As reported in *Time*, September 23, 1946, p. 53.

19 S. Hook, *Education for Modern Man* (New York: Dial Press, 1946), p. 66.

20 From an unpublished address.

21 National Catholic Education Association, *op. cit.*, p. 18.

22 J. B. Conant, *op. cit.*, p. 69.

either as faculty members, administrative officers, members of boards of trustees, or officials of religious organizations. While the Commission might well have presented in greater detail the historic role of private institutions in the development of higher education in the United States, their distinctive function in the present and future, and their pressing needs, it could not possibly have been unmindful of these matters. Certainly by no reasonable interpretation could the Commission be charged with antagonism to private education.

It has been said that under the program advocated by the Commission, private groups in many instances would probably be denied permission to establish new educational institutions. The Commission had no such intention. In fact, it made a strong avowal to the contrary, saying:

The responsibility for providing a strong system of public education does not, however, deny in any way to any individual or group of individuals the right to attend, or to establish and support in addition to public schools, a private or denominational institution for the purpose of providing, within limits prescribed by law, a kind of education which such individuals or groups deem more suitable to their particular needs and beliefs. It is just as undemocratic for the government to restrict in any way this fundamental right as it is for the government to fail to meet its prime responsibility for a strong system of public education.[23]

The accusation that the Commission hoped to set limits to the development of private higher education because it suggested that private institutions might be expected to take only about 900,000 students in 1960 simply does not hold

water. At the very time the Commission made its estimate, many private colleges and universities were announcing their intention to *reduce* enrollments as soon as the veteran bulge had passed. It is rather inconsistent, to say the least, for these institutions to complain at one moment that the Commission wanted to thwart their expansion and at the next instant to announce cutbacks in their attendance.

The private institutions may fear that increased expenditures for public higher education will make it more difficult to secure gifts for private colleges and universities. Even if this should prove to be true — and I think the fear is exaggerated — do these institutions wish to take the position that therefore no considerable expansion of educational opportunity at public expense should be countenanced? Such a position would create an unfortunate cleavage between public and private higher education. "Whenever that conflict arises in a democracy, as in the case of the grade schools and the high schools," President Turck has warned, "the public institutions win."[24] The history of education in the United States is the record of the people's determination steadily to make the advantages of education, first at elementary and secondary levels, and later at advanced levels, more freely and widely available. There is no likelihood that they will falter in that determination.

It is difficult to state just where the representatives of private institutions as a group stand on the question of federal financial aid to higher education. Some apparently are opposed to federal aid to either public or private institutions. Others seem to be anxious to secure federal assistance for general educational

---

[23] *Higher Education for American Democracy,* "Financing Higher Education," V, 57.

[24] C. J. Turck, *op. cit.*

purposes and plant expansion, but expect the government to provide the funds without holding the institutions accountable for the way in which they are spent. Nearly everyone supports in principle, if not in detail, the Commission's recommendations for a federal system of competitive scholarships and fellowships tenable at any accredited college or university.

The Commission decided, only two members dissenting, that the autonomy of private institutions could best be preserved and that the recognized principle of public responsibility for providing an educational system open to all on equal grounds could best be maintained, by making federal funds for general educational support and general capital outlay available only to public institutions. However, the Commission emphasized "the long established principle in America that the responsibility for education resides with the States" and recommended "that the determination of what institutions or systems of education are publicly controlled and thus eligible to receive public funds for the support of higher education, as recommended by this Commission, *should be left to the States*"[25] (italics mine).

The Commission's recommendations embody the prospect of considerable financial reinforcement of private colleges and universities. The scholarship and fellowship plan already mentioned should enable these institutions to maintain student bodies of appropriate size and quality. The Commission explicitly recommended that the Federal Government be free to make contracts with individual institutions, whether publicly or privately controlled, for specific services, including the capital outlay that may be

necessary in conducting them. Privately controlled universities at this moment are the recipients of large grants for both basic and applied research, and this program should be further strengthened and broadened when the National Science Foundation is established. Through aid for research, graduate education is indirectly supported. These universities thus receive assistance for the costliest portion of their activities. It should be noted, too, that the Commission assumed that contracts with private institutions could legitimately cover training as well as research. All in all, one can only interpret the Commission's proposals as holding out to independent colleges and universities the possibility of material benefit.

It is not necessary to debate the general principle of federal aid to education. The case for federal aid to the states on an equalization basis for elementary and secondary schools has been so well presented in many publications that it need not be summarized here. The extension of federal aid through the states to post high-school education can be supported on the same fundamental principles. "Those of us who believe the two-year community colleges are a significant step forward in the march of attaining our goal of equalizing educational opportunity," President Conant has written, "have high hopes that they will prosper in every state. . . . Without the use of the taxing power of the Federal government, however, there can be no adequate expansion of community colleges in many sections of the country."[26]

But what about the contention that undesirable political control from Washington will inevitably follow federal aid? Has the Commission recommended a

[25] *Op. cit.*, V, 58.

[26] J. B. Conant, *op. cit.*, pp. 201–3.

program which, if adopted, will ultimately impose statism on American education? It is possible to adduce the testimony of no small amount of experience on this question. "The Land-Grant colleges," President Jones has reminded us, "have some 80 years' experience with Federal aid and should know something about it. Federal aid has *not* resulted in Federal control. On the contrary, our Land-Grant college system is a remarkable example of decentralized control."27 The Federal Government has spent millions on the education of veterans, and practically everyone, I believe, would agree with President Conant that this method of channeling federal funds to both public and private institutions has not led to any trace of federal control.

"Federal funds should flow to the *state*," President Conant also has pointed out (and the Commission has recommended), "and be dispersed within the state by state authorities acting according to state law. If this principle is adhered to in any plan for Federal aid to schools, control of education from Washington by the most zealous bureaucrat will be almost impossible to achieve. Let it be noted carefully that the points of contact, so to speak, would be kept to forty-eight; no Federal funds would be involved at the school level."28

Whether federal funds in any form are distributed for educational purposes to either public or private institutions, the state agency, and ultimately the institution, receiving such funds will and should be held accountable to the *public* for using them in accordance with the broad purposes and general conditions under which they were granted. This is a thoroughly democratic principle. The people will always reserve the right to review

27 L. W. Jones, *op. cit.*

28 J. B. Conant, *op. cit.*, p. 191.

the integrity with which institutions use the funds they supply. The state colleges and universities are not responsible in this sense merely to their legislatures, but even more fundamentally to the citizens of their states, *to whom they also turn, if the necessity arises, for protection against partisan or injurious political domination or interference, or any other kind of unprincipled pressure.* Private institutions, too, in accepting such benefits as tax exemption, become accountable to the people for conducting their educational activities broadly in the public interest.

Although there have been unfortunate instances of political interference with state institutions, these occasions have grown increasingly rare, for to a remarkable degree, citizens have come to understand the necessity for freedom of teaching and research in their colleges and universities. Those of us who are staff members or members of boards of trustees of independent or church-related institutions know full well that private education is not completely free from the pressure of special interests and that their history is not entirely unmarred by instances of overt or subtle interference with academic freedom and the unfettered search for truth. Nevertheless, the Commission was undoubtedly sincere in its conviction that the cause of freedom from undesirable domination from whatever source is powerfully bolstered by the ideals and practices of colleges and universities which are independent of direct governmental support and public control. Both public and private institutions will derive increased strength and freedom from a pluralistic system.

A member of the Commission who signed the statement of dissent from the recommendation that federal funds for general educational purposes and general capital outlay should be granted only to public institutions, and who has also criticized the report on other grounds, has nevertheless stated in the following words the goal toward which all should strive: "The dominant idea in the Commission's Report is this: It is in keeping with the American tradition of democracy and in the best interests of the national welfare that every young American of good moral character should have the opportunity of profiting from higher education to the extent of his capacity. The idea is a great one, and it can and ought to be realized."[29]

Accepting the broad goal, let us continue to explore and discuss questions of method. For in the process of discussion, sound approaches to the ultimate objective are almost certain to be found, and the support of the American people for a forward-looking program almost sure to be enlisted.

[29] M. R. P. McGuire, mimeographed copy of an address on "The New Community College: Implications for Catholic Education."

Suggestions for Additional Reading

The first requisite for a fuller understanding of the issues involved in this controversy is to read more of the Report of the President's Commission, especially Vol. II, *Equalizing and Expanding Educational Opportunity,* and Vol. III, *Organizing Higher Education.*

A good introduction to further study of this problem, one which succinctly recounts the historical background out of which it emerges, is Charles A. Beard, *The Unique Function of Education in American Democracy* (Washington, D. C., 1937). Harold J. Laski's chapter on "American Education" in his *The American Democracy* (New York, 1948) gives an excellent brief description as well as a critical appraisal of our school system as a whole. The report of the American Youth Commission, *Youth and the Future* (Washington, D. C., 1942), shows clearly how present-day social and economic conditions generate the need and the demand for increased educational opportunity. Three sociologists, W. Lloyd Warner, Robert J. Havighurst, and Martin B. Loeb, have written in *Who Shall Be Educated?* (New York, 1944) a vividly realistic account of the way in which our schools serve to maintain and even reinforce a class stratification while at the same time they provide for a limited degree of social mobility. Elmo Roper made an interesting survey of public opinion for *Fortune* (Supplement, September, 1949) which discloses that a great majority of people want federal subsidies for increased educational opportunity, *and* that they want it chiefly for its supposed economic advantages. In view of these results of the *Fortune* poll, the careful study by Seymour E. Harris of *The Market for College Graduates* (Cambridge, 1949) assumes increased importance.

Some other valuable discussions of the role of higher education in our democracy are: Oliver Carmichael, *The Changing Role of Higher Education* (New York, 1949); James Bryant Conant, *Education in a Divided World: The Function of the Public Schools in Our Unique Society* (Cambridge, 1948); Ordway Tead, *Equalizing Educational Opportunities beyond the Secondary School* (Cambridge, 1947); Benjamin Fine, *Democratic Education* (New York, 1945); and the report of the Harvard Committee on General Education, *General Education in a Free Society* (Cambridge, 1945).

There is a voluminous literature on the subject of junior colleges and community colleges. James A. Starrak and Raymond M. Hughes in *The New Junior College: The Next Step in Free Public Education* (Ames, Iowa, 1948) briefly but trenchantly present the case for the extension of public education through the fourteenth grade. *The New American College* (New York, 1946) by John A. Sexson and John W. Harbeson gives a more detailed discussion, with particular attention to the highly developed system of public junior colleges in the state of California. John S. Diekhoff in *Democracy's College: Higher Education in the Local Community* (New York, 1950) argues for community colleges but against any form of federal aid that would impair the autonomy of local control.

Two educational periodicals devoted whole issues to a series of articles on the Report, the *Journal of Educational Sociology* (April, 1949) and the *Journal of Higher Education* (April, 1948). The latter contains a series of six articles, one on each of the six volumes of the Report.

Reactions to the Report by representatives of privately endowed institutions were mixed. A report of the Commission on Liberal Education to the Association of American Colleges (*Bulletin, Association of American Colleges,* 35, 1949, 159–162) disapproving some of the basic recommendations of the President's Commission, was, after an animated discussion, accepted by a majority of those present at the meeting. (For the action on this report, see the *Bulletin,* 35, 1949, 182–183.) Two articles by presidents of small colleges which respectively defend and attack the Report are: Harold Taylor, "The Future of American Education," *American Scholar,* 18 (1949), 33–40; and Gordon Keith Chalmers, "The Social Role of Education" (*Ibid.,* 41–49). Other articles which stress the concern of the privately endowed colleges and universities are: Paul Swain Havens, "Another Way Out?" *Journal of Educational Sociology*, 22 (1949), 522–532; W. H. Cowley, "Thoughts on the Truman Report," *Journal of Higher Education*, 19 (1948), 275–283; Russel D. Cole, "Freedom under Federal Aid to Education," *Bulletin, Association of American Colleges*, 35 (1949), 279–282. Robert M. Hutchins, "Education and Democracy," *School and Society*, 69 (1949), 425–482 and Byron S. Hollinshead, "The Report of the President's Commission on Higher Education," *Bulletin, American Association of University Professors*, 34 (1948), 257–271, extend and supplement the articles by them which are included in these readings. Harold Q. Voorhis, "Let's Stop Leaning on Washington," *School and Society*, 68 (1948), 377–380, is a vigorous protest against federal subsidies for education.

Two important groups of educational institutions affected by the recommendations in the Report are the Protestant, church-related colleges and the Catholic colleges and universities. Discussions of the Report by representatives of the first group are: G. C. White, "Church-Related Colleges and the Report of the President's Commission on Higher Education," *Bulletin, Association of American Colleges*, 34 (1948), 456–461; Gould Wickey, "The President Studies Higher Education," *Christian Education*, 31 (1948), 93–102; H. S. Sherwood, "Life or Death for Private Colleges?" *Christian Education*, 31 (1948), 103–109. The most detailed statement of criticisms from the Catholic point of view is the one made by a group of Catholic educators in the pamphlet *Whither American Education?* (New York, 1948), edited by Allan P. Farrell. A hostile review of this pamphlet by Paul Blanshard, entitled "Made in Rome," *Journal of Higher Education*, 20 (1949), 110–111, was answered by Robert C. Harnett, S.J., in a subsequent issue (*Ibid.*, 274–275 and 282). Other comments on the Report by Catholic writers are: Reverend John A. Ellert, "Equalizing Educational Opportunity in the Field of Higher Education," *Catholic Educational Review*, 46 (1948), 341–357, and Very Reverend Robert I. Gannon, "Relationships of Government and Religion to Education," *Proceedings, National Catholic Education Association* (Washington, 1949, 52–57).

The most comprehensive and thoroughgoing discussion of the problem of financing education is Seymour E. Harris, *How Shall We Pay for Education? Approaches to the Economics of Education* (New York, 1948). Frank Pace, Jr., while he was Director of the Bureau of the Budget, gave a brief but authoritative analysis of the financial problems involved in proposed plans for federal aid to education in "The Federal Government and Education," *Journal of Higher Education*, 21 (1950), 1–6 and 55. Two discussions of this aspect of the Report of the President's Commission are: Alfred D. Simpson, "Financing Higher Education," *Journal of Higher Education*, 19 (1948), 194–202 and 217–218, and H. K. Newburn, "The Financing of Public Education in the United States," *The Educational Record*, 30 (1949), 23–32. See also for this subject T. L. Hungate's *Financing the Future of Higher Education* (New York, 1946). A detailed survey of the multifarious ways in which the federal government is already supporting higher education is James Earl Russell's *Federal Activities in Higher Education after the Second World War* (New York, 1951).

In recent years there have been a number of important surveys of the programs of higher education in individual states. Representative studies are: Coleman R. Griffith, *The Junior College in Illinois* (Urbana, 1945); *Higher Education in Minnesota* (Minneapolis, 1950), a report by the Minnesota Commission on Higher Education; *Higher Education in Maryland* (Washington, D. C., 1947), a study by the Maryland Commission on Higher Education; *A Report of a Survey of the Needs of California in Higher Education* (Sacramento, 1948) by the California State Department of Education; and the *Report of the Temporary Commission on the Need for a State University in New York State* (Albany, 1948). In connection with this last report see also Charles M. Armstrong's *The Need for Higher Education in New York State* (Albany, 1948). An article by Alfred B. Bonds, "Implementing the Report of the President's Commission on Higher Education — A Case Study for Pennsylvania," *Educational Record*, 30 (1949), 93–104, indicates how the recommendations of the Report might be carried out in one particular state.